THEY

LOVED

THE

TORAH

Dedicated to my dear friend
Sgt. Eitan Messica, ל״ז (of blessed memory).

What
Yeshua's
First
Followers
Really
Thought
About
the Law

THEY

LOVED

THE

TORAH

David Friedman, Ph.D.

Lederer Books
a division of
Messianic Jewish Publishers
Clarksville, Maryland

Printed in the United States of America
Cover by Now You See it! graphics
Interior design by Drawing Board Studios

10 09 08 07   7 6 5 4
ISBN-10: 1-880226-94-4
ISBN-13: 978-1-880226-94-0

Library of Congress Catalog Control Number: 2001092014

Lederer Books
a division of
Messianic Jewish Publishers
P.O. Box 615
Clarksville, Maryland 21029

Distributed by
Messianic Jewish Resources International
Order line: (800) 410-7367
E-mail: lederer@messianicjewish.net
Website: www.messianicjewish.net

CONTENTS

FOREWORD

When scholars can capture the complexities of theology and biblical content in down-to-earth language, there is power and beauty. This is one of the best characteristics of Dr. David Friedman's book, *They Loved the Torah*. The truth he is espousing is that the Torah (the first five books of the Bible) occupied a central place in the earthly life of Yeshua the Messiah, as well as in the lives of all of his followers, including *Sha'ul* (Paul) of Tarsus. Dr. Friedman's findings can be easily grasped.

The loyalty that Yeshua and his students had toward the Torah is evident from even a cursory reading of the pages of the Newer Covenant Scriptures. Dr. Friedman makes that truth even more clear in this book. That over the centuries, many godly and sincere scholars have missed seeing the Torah faithfulness of Yeshua and his students (who later were the writers of Scripture themselves), is an amazing fact. They have asserted, instead, that Yeshua's atoning death and miraculous Resurrection rendered the Torah inoperative. Furthermore, they have taught that since Yeshua fulfilled the Torah, his followers (including us, today) have no responsibility to live it. Moreover, when it comes to *Sha'ul*, the typical conclusion among many Pauline scholars is, as Dr. Cheryl Ann Brown asserted in her foreword to Brad Young's book, *Paul, the Jewish Theologian*, "In many people's minds, Paul remains the 'founder' of Christianity and is cut off almost . . . from his Jewish roots." *They Loved the Torah* is Dr. Friedman's significant contribution to the modern reassessment of these historical theological conclusions.

In recent years, there has been a movement among many believers to take another look at the Torah and its place in the daily lives of those who trust in Yeshua. There are a growing number of voices rising in opposition to the accepted, centuries-long anti-Torah position of the majority of those who claim to follow Yeshua. In this book, Friedman has successfully demonstrated the deep love that Yeshua and his *talmidim* (students)—including *Sha'ul* of Tarsus—had for the first five books of the Bible. Dr. Friedman has amassed clear and irrefutable evidence from the Scriptures that the Torah was more than just a book of Messianic typology to the first-century believers. Rather, Dr. Friedman has drawn the natural conclusions that have somehow escaped many Bible scholars through the centuries about the place the Torah occupied in the lives of Yeshua and his first followers. He observes that they provided living and loving examples to follow for all of us who believe in him. He has accomplished all of this in clear, down to earth language. The research can feed the scholars; the language is palatable for the laymen.

It is my hope that all who read this book, whether Jewish or non-Jewish, will see the mass of evidence for Torah faithfulness accumulated by Dr. Friedman. May they be challenged to re-think their attitudes toward Torah for believers in Yeshua. *They Loved the Torah* contains not only sound scholarship (the basis of this book was Dr. Friedman's Ph.D. dissertation), but it is also written by a humble Jewish scholar, one who loves both the Living Torah (Yeshua), as well as the written Torah. Our family and his have been coworkers and close friends for several years. Truly, we can say of them that, just like Yeshua and his followers, they also love the Torah.

—Ariel Berkowitz
Congregational Leader, Kehilat Neve Tzion, Israel

PREFACE

Entering the world of the Torah is a privilege. When we study and discuss the Torah, we enter the world that many biblical figures, scholars, rabbis, and Messianic Jews entered as they attempted to learn about God. As I enter the world of the Torah through this book, I want to relay to you, the reader, my thorough respect and love for the Torah. Examining the meaning of the Torah for our day is a rich and meaningful experience. This is especially the case when we look at the Torah in the lives of the first generation of Messianic Jews. Therefore, it is with a sense of awe that I begin this essay.

It is my hope that the reader will understand how Yeshua and his first followers in Israel, including *Sha'ul* (Paul), *Shim'on* (Peter) and *Ya'akov* (James) related to the Torah. This is crucial if the reader desires to know what Yeshua taught and how he lived. Without understanding Yeshua's relation to the Torah, we will neither understand *what* he taught or *how* he lived his life. Furthermore, we will not know *why* he taught and lived as he did. To understand how Yeshua related to the Torah is relevant for all students of the Bible, whether Jewish or non-Jewish, as this is the base on which Yeshua built his life. Whether the reader is a student of first-century history, wanting to assess Yeshua's historical background, or is simply interested in developing personal religious awareness, this essay is relevant.

It is necessary to give you my working definition of the Torah. As I use the term *Torah*, I am referring to the first five books of the Scriptures—the books of Genesis, Exodus, Leviticus, Numbers, and Deuteronomy. It would be wrong to define the Torah as *Law*, as is done so often by commentators, translators, and teachers. The richness of the Torah is evidenced by its makeup—narrative history, instructions, instructional songs and poems, legal codes, genealogies, ethical instructions, and covenants. The fuller meaning of the term *Torah* refers to the full instruction given by God to the Jewish people, in what became known as the Scriptures. Each time the Torah is referred to in this book, however, its meaning is the instruction of God given in the first five books of Moses. This includes the legal codes, commandments, and statutes that we associate with the word *Law*. Additionally, the glossary in the back of this book will help the reader with some unfamiliar Hebrew terms. I suggest reviewing it before starting to read.

Finally, I wish to express my thanks to the following people for their help in the writing of this book: Dr. John Fischer, Ariel Berkowitz, L. Savage, H. Weiss, and last but certainly not least, M. Friedman, without whose encouragement this work would not exist.

PART ONE

YESHUA AND THE TORAH

CHAPTER ONE

THE TORAH OBSERVANCE OF YESHUA'S FAMILY

The keys to understanding Yeshua's Torah observance are two-fold. First, we will see that he kept the Torah's commandments. Then, we will see that his teachings mirrored his practice. In some sense, I am making this artificial division because every rabbi of that era taught through both practice and oral teaching as an integrated whole. After we see Yeshua's words and example, such an integrated whole will emerge.[1]

As we examine Yeshua's Torah observance, it is logical to look at his family background. It is important to understand how Yeshua was brought up. If his family was Torah-observant, then we should expect that Yeshua would have been Torah-observant as well. His upbringing would have been rich with the study of the Torah, the keeping of the feasts and holidays, and a deep connection to the history and calling of the nation of Israel. Let us see what the evidence shows us.

Yeshua's Family Upbringing

When we study the scriptural information about Yeshua's home life, it soon becomes evident that his family brought him up as a Torah-observant Jew. The family fit into the normal range of Torah observance for their era and geographic location (first century C.E. Galilean Judaism). This is seen from Yeshua's earliest days. In Luke 2:21–32, Yeshua and his family fulfilled the *mitzvah* of circumcision as found in Exodus 13:2, 11–16 and Leviticus 12:1–8. The Leviticus text states:

> When a woman gives birth to a boy ... he is to be circumcised on the eighth day ... and when the days of purification pass ... bring a one-year old sheep for a burnt offering, and a dove or

pigeon for a sin offering, to the entrance of the Tent of Meeting, to the *kohen* . . . or bring two pigeons or two doves, one for a burnt offering and one for a sin offering; and the *kohen* will perform the atonement and purification ceremony. (author's translation)

The text in Luke shows the literal fulfillment of this *mitzvah* by Joseph and Miriam (Mary), Yeshua's parents.

On the eighth day, when it was time for his *b'rit-milah* [circumcision], he was given the name Yeshua. . . . [T]hey took him up to Yerushalayim [Jerusalem] to present him to ADONAI (as it is written in the *Torah* of ADONAI, "Every firstborn male is to be consecrated to ADONAI") and also to offer a sacrifice of a pair of doves or two young pigeons, as required by the *Torah* of ADONAI. (Luke 2:21–24)

Yeshua was circumcised according to the *mitzvot* of the Mosaic (and Abrahamic) Covenant(s). The Greek phrase, κατα τον νομον Μοσευς *(kata ton nomon Moseus,* according to the Torah of Moses), in Luke 2:22, makes it clear that Yeshua's family did this in order to fulfill the requirements of the Torah. Luke 2:24, explains that the sacrifice offered by the family was the one mentioned in Leviticus 12:8. Here is one clear example of the Torah-observant ways of Yeshua's family. In addition, it is doubtful that the righteous man of Luke 2:25, meaning a strict Torah-observant Jew, would bless the Messiah (v. 28) if the Messiah was not going to be Torah-observant. A *tzaddik* would not give this blessing to a Torah-ignorant person. It is hardly conceivable, based on any Jewish writings or rabbinic literature with which I am familiar, that the Messiah would not observe the Torah. The text makes it clear why Yeshua and his family came to Jerusalem in this instance: "to do for him [Yeshua] what the Torah required" (v. 27b).

Indeed, the family's scrupulous Torah observance is shown in Luke 2:39: "Yosef and Miryam [Joseph and Mary] . . . finished doing everything required by the *Torah.*" Both the Greek text and the corresponding Hebrew translations bring out the beautiful flavor of this phrase, which well portrays the fact that Joseph and Miriam were careful to fulfill all of the *mitzvot* of the Torah regarding the birth, ritual cleansing period, circumcision, and sacrifices for their newborn son. This alone tells us a good deal about the family atmosphere in which Yeshua was raised. His family was not abnormal. As Dr. Safrai noted in his lecture of December 16, 1996, in Jerusalem, Israel, a Torah-observant home environment was normal for a Galilean Jewish family of that period. Logic, culture, and history dictate that Yeshua grew up as a Torah-observant child and youth. At age twelve, we find Yeshua fulfilling a *mitzvah* of the Torah with his family. Luke 2:41 states, "Every year Yeshua's parents went to Yerushalayim for the festival of Pesach [Passover]." It is evident that participating in the pilgrimage festivals was the custom of Yeshua's family. As with all Jews of that time, this was done out of obedience to the *mitzvot* of the Torah. Here, the family fulfilled the *mitzvah* found in Exodus 23:14–15 and Deuteronomy 16:16. The Deuteronomy text states, "Three times a year all your men are to appear [in Yerushalayim] in the presence of ADONAI your God . . . [including] at the festival of *matzah* [unleavened bread/Passover]." Yeshua's family kept the festival cycle outlined in Leviticus 23.

On this particular Passover pilgrimage, the twelve-year-old Yeshua showed his desire to serve God and to know the true meaning of the Torah. He spent three full days in discussion of the Torah with leading Jerusalem rabbis (see Luke 2:43–50). If Yeshua, or his family for that matter, had been hostile to observing the Torah, this pilgrimage event would not have occurred. It is highly unlikely that Yeshua would have engaged in a three-day discussion about the Torah with rabbis if he had held an anti-Torah attitude. Although it is impossible to identify these Jerusalem rabbis, they may have been Sanhedrin members. Leading Sanhedrin members headed *yeshivas*, or religious schools, where they taught young Jewish boys and men about the Torah. To engage in discussion of the Torah with a young Jewish pilgrim from Galilee is very imaginable. In Luke 2, could Yeshua have discussed the Torah with such eminent teachers as the sages Hillel, Shammai, or *Rabban Gamliel (Sha'ul's teacher)*? We do not know. Yet, it does remain within the realm of historical possibility that this happened. No matter who these rabbis actually were, it is hardly possible that three days worth of discussions could have taken place between such lovers of the Torah and Yeshua, had Yeshua not been Torah-observant.[2]

As a youth, Yeshua is also portrayed as fulfilling Exodus 20:12, which states, "Honor your father and mother." Luke 2:51 notes that Yeshua "went with them [his parents] to Natzeret [Nazareth] and was obedient to them." Yeshua was obedient to his parents, thereby fulfilling more of the Torah's instructions. Although Exodus 20:12 is not mentioned specifically in Luke 2:51, Yeshua's actions did fulfill this *mitzvah*.

Rabbi Harvey Falk states, "He [Yeshua] strengthened the Torah of Moses majestically . . . not one of our sages spoke out more emphatically concerning the immutability of the Torah."[3]

Yeshua's Torah-Observant Cousin

It is appropriate to determine if Yeshua's relatives were Torah-observant, as this would strengthen the picture of the extended family being devoted to fulfilling the Torah. The Scriptures are relatively silent regarding this issue. However, one of Yeshua's relatives, his cousin John, is portrayed in a Torah-observant light.

In Mark 6:17–20, we have our relevant text. Yeshua's cousin John the Baptist is murdered for his devotion to the Torah. Due to his love for God, he had rebuked King Herod Antipas, who had disobeyed the *mitzvah* of Leviticus 18:16: "You are not to have sexual relations with your brother's wife, because that is your brother's prerogative."

John reproved the king for breaking this *mitzvah* (see Mark 6:18). Although Antipas murdered him in return, the king feared John and considered him a *tzaddik*, or righteous man. In the historical context of this event, it took a very Torah-zealous person to rebuke Herod Antipas, as it was a dangerous act to perform. This king had the power to kill John if he was insulted by his rebuke. John's motivation was one of devotion to God and to God's Torah. It is of note that the term used in the Greek New Testament (Mark 6:20) to refer to John is ανδρα δικαιον (*andra dikaion*). This is the probable Greek cognate term corresponding to the Hebrew technical term, צדיק (the aforementioned word, *tzaddik*). Indeed, John's students are elsewhere described as fasting and praying often: "The disciples of John often fast and offer prayers, the disciples of the Pharisees also do the same" (Luke 5:33 NASB). If John's students lived in this manner, it is logical that they learned to do so from John. John understood that he was a forerunner to Yeshua, who would have even greater influence. In fact, he stated, "After me One is coming who is mightier than I, and I am not fit to stoop down and untie the thong of his sandals" (Mark 1:7 NASB).

If, according to Mark 6:20, John was a *tzaddik*, Yeshua would have been one all the more so—being as scrupulously Torah-observant as his cousin was. I therefore conclude that, since John was uncompromisingly Torah-observant, even unto death, Yeshua would also have been so. The two men were from the same family, and should have been consistent in the manner in which they approached Torah observance. The record bears this out.

Additionally, Luke 1:6 sheds light on the manner of Torah observance of John's parents: "Both of them [John's parents] were righteous before God, observing all the *mitzvot* and ordinances of *Adonai* blamelessly." In this verse, the Greek word δικαιοι (*dikaioi*) is used in describing John's parents, Zechariah and Elizabeth. This is the same Greek word as in Mark 6:20, where the text spoke of John as being a *tzaddik*.

Let us remember that the Hebrew word *tzaddik* means a scrupulously Torah-observant person. John was raised in this manner, with parents who were zealous toward fulfilling the *mitzvot*. As mentioned earlier, John was arrested and later murdered when he reproved the king for breaking the Torah. The picture that we see of John and his parents, then, is one of devotion to keeping and teaching the Torah.

After examining the evidence, we can conclude that Yeshua was brought up in a Torah-observant atmosphere. His immediate family, as evidenced by his parents' lives, was Torah-observant. His broader family, as evidenced by the lives of his cousins (from the house of Zechariah the priest), was also Torah-observant. The New Testament paints this picture for us. In short, we can readily see that Yeshua's family brought him up to observe the *mitzvot* of the Torah.

CHAPTER TWO

YESHUA AND HIS SABBATH OBSERVANCE

Central to showing Yeshua's Torah-observant life is an understanding of his observance of the Sabbath (see Exod. 20:8; 23:12–13; Lev. 23:3). Sabbath observance was considered a prime duty and crucial *mitzvah* in the Second Temple era. Whatever particular wing of Judaism a person may have adhered to in this period, all Jewry looked upon the keeping of the Sabbath as extremely important.

How Did Yeshua Keep the Sabbath?

The evidence from the New Covenant clearly indicates that Yeshua kept the Sabbath (see Matt. 5:17–20; Luke 4:16–22, 31). Therefore, the question to be considered is not whether Yeshua kept the Sabbath, but rather, "In what manner did he keep it?" Our conclusions will uphold the main assertion of this book: Yeshua lived an undeniably Torah-observant lifestyle.

How is it that Yeshua actually kept the Sabbath if he received so much opposition from religious teachers concerning his Sabbath observance? (Please refer to Luke 6:1–11; John 7:22–24; and John 9:16 for examples of this opposition.) Jewish sources differ as to if and how Yeshua transgressed the *mitzvah* of Sabbath observance. However, most sources agree that Yeshua had differences with various movements of the Israeli Jewish world of his time.

Four well known scholars—Klausner, Montefiore, Abrahams, and Cohen—have asserted that Yeshua violated the *mitzvah* of keeping the Sabbath, while two other scholars—Jacobs and Schonfeld—asserted that he did not break any scriptural *mitzvot* regarding the Sabbath. Still four others—Kohler, Flusser, Lapide, and Vermes—asserted that he did not violate scriptural *mitzvot*, nor did he have any major differences with accepted Pharisaic Sabbath keeping.[1] Indeed, Kohler suggested that the whole Sabbath conflict regarding Yeshua could be understood in light of the arguments of Rabbi Hillel with Rabbi Shammai concerning how to correctly fulfill the Sabbath *mitzvot*.

One of the most influential Second Temple period scholars of our time, Shmuel Safrai, noted that Yeshua kept the Sabbath fully according to the *halakhah* of his day. Commenting upon Yeshua's Sabbath observance, Dr. Safrai stated, "It was 100 percent according to the Law."[2] Vermes agreed with him: "[Yeshua's] basic attitudes [toward the Sabbath] . . . are the same as those of the rabbis."[3] I believe, following Flusser, Lapide, and Vermes, that Yeshua did not break any scriptural *mitzvot* concerning the Sabbath. His differences with various religious leaders, as outlined in the New Covenant, should be understood as typical of the world of first-century Judaism.

Historical Background on Sabbath Observance

Many examples of this type of halakhic conflict are to be found in the rabbinic literature of the first century B.C.E. As mentioned above, the religious schools of Rabbi Hillel and Rabbi Shammai—both well within the Pharisaic tradition—are said to have had over 300 points of contention between them concerning how to fulfill the Torah. In other words, these rabbis and their students were allies with each other, yet they daily argued, debated, and struggled with each other over the most important issue in life to all of them—understanding the Torah. Yeshua simply took part in this struggle. Often, these differences of opinion, as in Yeshua's case, took on proportions of life and death. We have an example of these differences in the Talmud. Rabbi Tarfon was traveling and stopped to pray, praying after the manner taught by Rabbi Shammai.

> Rabbi Tarfon said, "I was travelling on the road and I reclined to recite the Shema [a special prayer], according to the ruling of Bet Shammai. Robbers came, endangering me . . . [so I fled]." His colleagues told him, "You would have deserved what you would have gotten [death] for not adhering to Bet Hillel's ruling [on how to pray]." (*Mishnah Berakhot* 1:3)

Those Pharisaic rabbis who adhered to Rabbi Hillel's teaching on prayer had no sympathy for Tarfon in his near escape from death at the hand of bandits, since Tarfon prayed according to Rabbi Shammai's custom. This reaction to Tarfon's predicament illustrates the seriousness of interpretational differences among allies in the first century. In part, this is because interpretational differences involved political differences. In the above situation, the Second Temple had already fallen (70 c.e.). The Israeli city of Yavneh had absorbed many refugee Pharisees. Various Pharisaic schools of thought were jockeying for the head position from which to lead the Jewish people through this difficult period of Roman oppression. Whomever you followed in terms of Torah interpretation was the one whose movement you supported in terms of political power. This was unavoidable. Certainly, there were genuine points of interpretational conflict. However, the motivation of the Yavneh rabbis was to follow God and preserve the Jewish people.

Many other halakhic conflicts portrayed in the Talmud, although too numerous to mention, can be seen in this light.[4] Such doctrinal and political differences were a definite part of Yeshua's arguments with some Pharisees. We will see that the doctrinal and political differences, as in Rabbi Tarfon's case, very much influenced the severity of the conflict between Yeshua and the authorities that argued with him. In fact, Safrai noted that in Second Temple times verbal sparring among rabbis was a common, accepted practice. This was particularly true between Galilean and Judean religious authorities. Safrai commented that Galilee, where Yeshua was educated and raised, was actually more devoted, as a whole, to the study and practice of the Torah than many parts of Judah.[5] Some of Yeshua's arguments with the religious authorities in Judah were common to the rivalry between Galilean and Judean religious teachers of this era. In fact, both Safrai and Young feel that Yeshua's approach to the Torah was close to that of the "Hasidic" movement of his day.[6]

Case in Point: The *Shabbat*

Let us examine the scriptural evidence of Yeshua's Sabbath observance (see Matt. 12:9; Mark 1:21; 6:2; Luke 4:16, 31; 6:6; 13:10; 14:1; John 5:1–16; John 9). In all of these narratives Yeshua is either in synagogue on the Sabbath or is teaching on the Sabbath. Luke 4:16 and 4:31 indicate that it was Yeshua's custom to pray in synagogue on every Sabbath, observing this day according to local custom. Luke 4:16 says, "On *Shabbat* he [Yeshua] went to the synagogue as usual." This shows us what he normally did on the Sabbath. Luke 4:31 confirms this: "[Yeshua] made a practice of teaching them on *Shabbat*."

Let us look at some examples of Yeshua's *Shabbat* observance that have been brought into question, both by his contemporaries as well as by many interpreters down through the centuries.

Healing and Handling the Sick

Mark mentions the timing of one of Yeshua's acts of healing: "That evening after sundown, they brought to Yeshua all who were ill or held in the power of demons" (1:32). The verse emphasizes that Yeshua publicly healed during what is termed מוצאי שבת (Hebrew, *motza'ey Shabbat*), that is, after the official passing of the Sabbath. This was done to insure keeping the oral traditions around the Sabbath concerning the transport of invalid persons. Although what customs were kept then is not revealed, we can make an educated guess about the general sentiment of the time. Lachs, commenting upon this verse, noted, "The people waited until evening [*motza'ey Shabbat*] to carry out their sick to him [Yeshua], and thus avoiding desecrating the Shabbat by carrying them, an act which was forbidden."[7]

It is also true that at other times (and as a principle) Yeshua healed people on the Sabbath (see Mark 1:29–31). The issue was not whether healing could take place on the Sabbath (see John 5:1–16; 9:13–14). In both of these instances, Yeshua taught that healing could take place on the Sabbath, according to the ruling of *Beyt Hillel*. The issue was whether he would authorize and allow the transportation of sick people on the Sabbath.[8]

Put differently, the issue is whether Yeshua had the authority to teach anything other than the accepted custom concerning the transportation of sick people on the Sabbath. To know the answer to this, the exact identity of Yeshua's opposition in John 5 and John 9 is crucial. Although we do not know who these people were, they undoubtedly held to the opinion of *Beyt Shammai* on this issue. Yeshua did not agree with them. (It is possible that this opposition came from one or more of Shammai's second-generation *yeshiva*s, which held much political power among the Pharisees in these years.)

The Sabbath healing texts of the New Testament present a difficult problem concerning understanding how Yeshua observed the Sabbath. Yet, one thing is certain: Yeshua is recorded as having observed it, and he entered into many arguments on how to correctly keep it. As Parkes noted, "The sphere of disagreement was the sphere of the development of halachah.... It is not the observance of the Sabbath itself which is at issue."[9]

Halakhic Argumentation Regarding the Sabbath

Matthew 12:1–8 provides another example of how Yeshua kept the Sabbath. In verse 2, Yeshua was accused of teaching his students to break the Sabbath. He countered the accusation with what is known as a rabbinic קל וחומר (Hebrew, *kal vachomer*) argument.[10] He then backed his answer with two scriptural proofs. By doing this, he demonstrated that the customs and *avot*[11] that his accusers accepted had corrupted the correct order of priorities on the Sabbath. Perhaps what infuriated Yeshua's opponents, more than his actual halakhic argumentation, was the claim he made in verse 6, "I tell you, there is in this place something greater than the Temple."

This point was central to Yeshua's argument. These particular Pharisees probably perceived it as an outrageous, almost ridiculous comment, but it changed the essence of the argument from how to keep the Sabbath to Yeshua's true identity. The point to be made is that Yeshua argued for the setting of proper priorities on the Sabbath. His argumentation is halakhic and normal for first-century Judaism. A few years before Yeshua was an adult, Rabbis Hillel and Shammai argued fervently with each other for their understanding of the Torah, yet few would question their loyalty to it. Their students also argued against each other regarding their distinct interpretations of the Torah, yet no responsible scholar could question their loyalty to keeping it. Here is an example of this type of halakhic argumentation.

> Olives and grapes that have turned hard, the school of Shammai declare susceptible to uncleanness, but the school of Hillel declare them insusceptible. The school of Shammai declare black cummin insusceptible to uncleanness, and the school of Hillel declare it susceptible. So, too, do they differ concerning whether it is liable to tithes. (Danby edition, *Mishnah Uktzin* 2:6)

On the issue of ritual uncleanness, *Beyt Hillel* and *Beyt Shammai* differed regarding the categorizing of olives, grapes, and black cummin, as well as what items were liable for tithing. More examples of *Beyt Hillel-Beyt Shammai* argumentations are found in the Talmud. In fact, this passionate halakhic argumentation did, on occasion, lead to changes of opinion regarding how to fulfill the Torah. Such argumentation was valuable in formulating *halakhah*. Here is an example of such a change of opinion.

> If a woman returned from beyond the sea [abroad] and said, "My husband is dead," she may marry again; and if she said, "My husband died childless," she may contract levirate marriage. So [teaches] the school of Shammai. And the school of Hillel say: we have heard no such tradition save of a woman that returned from the harvest. The school of Shammai answered: It is all one (the same set of circumstances), whether she returned from the harvest or from the olive-picking or from beyond the sea . . . the school of Hillel changed their opinion and taught according to the school of Shammai. (Danby edition, *Mishnah Eduyot* 1:12a)

In the above incident, the argumentation between the *yeshiva*s of Hillel and Shammai led to *Beyt Hillel* changing its opinion, and changing the way they would fulfill this aspect of *halakhah*. After *Beyt Shammai*'s representatives argued their case to *Beyt Hillel*'s representatives, both Pharisaic schools accepted the opinion that a woman could remarry upon her own testimony, either freely or according to the Deuteronomy 25:5 levirate marriage law. The halakhic argumentation that took place served to provide a way for the two schools to get their teachings and reasoning heard. Their goal was to influence the developing *halakhah*. In all of this halakhic disputation, the main motivation was the desire to fulfill the Torah.

Similarly, in Matthew 12, Yeshua was arguing for the correct manner in which to keep the Sabbath. It is not reasonable to think that he intended, in any way, to break the Sabbath—because then he would have had to break the Torah. The type of argumentation found in Matthew 12 demonstrates the way in which the Jewish world of the first century taught the proper method of understanding and fulfilling the Torah. Clearly, Yeshua was doing just that, arguing fervently about how to fulfill the Torah and how to correctly understand the Torah's requirements and priorities.

Plucking Grain

A few matters remain to be discussed concerning this issue. Regarding the incident just cited, Rabbi Safrai noted, "Yeshua entered into a halakhic argument and gave his reasoning. He did not break the Sabbath."[12] Rabbi Safrai also observed that Yeshua and his students did not actually pluck the grain. He reasoned that no group of people would enter into or trample upon an uncut field of grain, as it was not legal to do so. However, Safrai noted that it is legal to enter such a grain field if the crops were already cut. Then, all who desire to do so, can enter, pick up grain lying on the ground, husk it in their hands, and eat. In fact, the Torah allows such a practice.

> Now when you reap the harvest of your land, you shall not reap to the very corners of your field, nor shall you gather the gleanings of your harvest. Nor shall you glean your vineyard, nor shall you gather the fallen fruit of your vineyard; you shall leave them for the needy and for the stranger. I am the Lord your God. (Lev. 19:9–10 NASB)

Rabbi Safrai understood that Yeshua's students, instead of plucking the grain, picked up already cut grain off the ground. The *Complete Jewish Bible* correctly states, "They began picking heads of grain and eating them" (Matt. 12:1). Picking heads of grain (off the ground, or off the stem, which was probably on the ground) is what Safrai understood to be happening in the text.[13] Interestingly, the Talmud records a situation where we can see the different positions Jews held concerning this halakhic issue.

> The men of Jericho did six things: for three they were reproved, and for three, they were not reproved. . . . [The sages did not reprove them when] they reaped and stacked [ripe barley] before the Omer. [The sages did reprove them when] they ate from fallen fruit on the Sabbath. (*Pesachim* 4:8)

Here, we can see the difference in the interpretation of proper *halakhah* between the Jews of Jericho and the stricter rabbis. The Jews of Jericho did not see any halakhic fault with eating fallen fruit on the Sabbath, yet the rabbis did. Here, the differences in halakhic interpretation are regional. Jericho, in the Jordan Valley, depended upon fruit for sustenance and economic life. *Pesachim* 4:8 probably refers to incidents around the time of Passover. Therefore, the issue being brought up is similar to the one in Matthew 12.

What was permitted halakhically regarding eating produce on the Sabbath? It is important for us to see that this kind of argumentation and regional understanding was standard for that day and age. First, who were these particular Pharisees that were out on this Sabbath, observing Yeshua and his students in the Matthew 12 text? Were they sent from Jerusalem to spy out the actions of the Galilean rabbi? Were they, perhaps, young, zealous *yeshiva* students eager to engage Yeshua in debate? Were they sent to find promising Galilean students to become their disciples and party members? Were they teachers and rabbis passing through the region, en route from teaching in one synagogue to the next? Or, were they strict adherents to the teachings of *Beyt Shammai*?

If we knew their identity, we could better understand the nature of their charges against Yeshua. My guess is that they were zealous young Pharisee party members from one of the Jerusalem academies, sent to assess the ritual state of Galilean Jews and to find promising candidates for instruction back in Jerusalem. Even if they were Pharisees who lived in the Galilee, this incident is very believable. Among Galilean sages themselves, there was an argument as to what was permitted regarding the husking, then eating, of grain on the Sabbath.[14]

Made for Man

Yeshua made another point that could easily have been understood as controversial, but would hardly have been grounds on which to establish a charge of Sabbath breaking. In Matthew 12:8, Yeshua asserted that human beings have authority over the Sabbath. In addition, he inferred that he, as Messiah, had the right to teach the true means of keeping the Sabbath and define its priorities. Yeshua pointed out that mankind, collectively, is king over the Sabbath, and that this order should not be reversed. Therefore, the Sabbath should serve man. Man should not be enslaved by attempting to live according to various opinions concerning correct Sabbath observance.

In Mark's version of this incident, Yeshua stated the same point: "Then he said to them, '*Shabbat* was made for mankind, not mankind for *Shabbat*. So the Son of Man is Lord even of *Shabbat*'" (2:27–28). Verse 28 expands upon the principle stated in verse 27. I understand Yeshua to be saying that collectively, men rule over the Sabbath. Yeshua, as a special "Son of Man" (in Second Temple language, "son of man" denoted an apocalyptic figure, or the Messiah), had authority from God to teach the Jewish people about correct Sabbath priorities. This incident demonstrates that Yeshua honored the Sabbath by defending it—by arguing for its true meaning. He stood up for what he considered proper priority setting for Sabbath observance.

Yeshua's understanding of man's relationship to the Sabbath was consistent with that of many rabbis of his time. As Vermes wrote, "[The idea that] the Sabbath was made for man, not man for the Sabbath, is also firmly rooted in rabbinic thought. . . . Sabbath observance in the second century, and probably also in the first, was subservient to the essential well-being of a Jew."[15]

A merciful, grace-full keeping of the Sabbath with proper scriptural priorities was not a new concept introduced by Yeshua. This was God's original intention in giving the Sabbath to the Jewish people. Yeshua, however, heard, saw, and experienced wrong teaching as to how to keep the Sabbath. The Gospel narratives show us that Yeshua, as the Messiah of Israel, passionately taught about correct Sabbath keeping. Other rabbis of his day and age did the same. The one difference is that Yeshua made a Messianic claim and taught that his teaching (or interpretation) was authoritative. This was the claim that caused much friction.

Shabbat: To Do Good

Matthew 12:9–15 is another passage of Scripture where we can see Yeshua's attitude toward keeping the Sabbath. Here, he was accused of violating some unidentified group's customs of healing on the Sabbath. Again, with a rabbinic *kal vachomer* argument,[16] he debated his accusers, giving them the correct understanding of Sabbath priorities. Verse 12 stands out as his "umbrella" teaching here: "Therefore, what is permitted on *Shabbat* is to do good."

A few observations may help us to see why the Pharisees wanted to "do away" with Yeshua (see v. 14). First, the accusers wanted to frame Yeshua for some type of serious Torah violation (see v. 10b for insight into their aim). Their question regarding healing may have been a lead-in, or trap, to get Yeshua to debate them. It may also have been designed to force Yeshua into contradicting their understanding of permissible Sabbath healings. Whatever their motive, we should read this situation as a confrontation between Yeshua and these particular Pharisees. These Pharisees did not represent the viewpoint of all Israel. Verse 15 shows that Yeshua was popular with the common people, while he threatened the popularity, mission, and authority of these particular Pharisees. As much as he was a threat to their perception of proper Jewish Sabbath practice, he was an even greater political threat. This aspect of the confrontation should not be underestimated, especially as it relates to the role it played in Yeshua's eventual death. Yeshua made enemies in high places, as evidenced by this particular group of Pharisees.

In Mark's version of this incident (3:1–6), allies of King Herod Antipas (son of Herod the First) joined with these angered Pharisees (see Luke 6:11) to form a plot to kill Yeshua. Antipas ruled over a smaller area than his father did. Likewise, Mark 3:6 emphasizes the political aspect of the conflict at hand. This conflict had more to do with the struggle between these Pharisees and Yeshua's perceived influence and role than it did with the question of how the Sabbath was to be observed. Yeshua and King Herod Antipas were at odds regarding their basic concepts of life. In Luke 13:32, Yeshua called Antipas *a fox*. In rabbinic literature, a fox represents a puffed-up buffoon who thinks he has great power (but in reality has little, if any). Antipas would have taken Yeshua's comment, in spite of its truth, as a curious and hard insult. In this same verse, Yeshua told Antipas what real power was: the ability to defeat death and rise again on the third day. For Antipas, power lay in his ability to please the Roman superpower and to spy on his people, controlling them by forceful means. This gives us some insight into a powerful enemy that Yeshua made, and why Antipas did not help Yeshua as he was facing death by Roman hands. In Luke 23:11–12, we see that Antipas used Yeshua's death as a means to befriend the Roman governor, Pontius Pilate. Yeshua was a political steppingstone for Antipas. Luke states that Antipas treated Yeshua with contempt (see v. 11). In standing up for the Torah, Yeshua made an enemy of the Herodian king, much as his cousin John had done before him.

Unloosing Oxen

Luke 13:10–17 is another Sabbath healing narrative. Here, Yeshua healed a handicapped woman, and was opposed by the chief synagogue official.

> But the president of the synagogue, indignant that Yeshua had healed on the *Shabbat*, spoke up and said to the congregation, "There are six days in the week for working; so come during those days to be healed, not on *Shabbat*" (v. 14).

This official understood that one could only receive healing on a weekday (Hebrew, יום חול, *yom hol*). On the Sabbath, healing was forbidden. This, in particular, reflects a pro-Shammaite view of healing on the Sabbath. Remember that Rabbi Shammai founded one of the Pharisaic schools of thought in Jerusalem, a generation or so before Yeshua. Here, Yeshua was teaching again on the proper priorities during the Sabbath. Probably, Yeshua is opposing the Shammaite school's understanding of the Sabbath. Commenting on Yeshua's healings on the Sabbath, Rabbi Safrai stated, "There was no *halakhah* against it!"[17] In fact, Safrai suggested that perhaps the head synagogue official was not as learned in the Sabbath *halakhah* as was Yeshua. Safrai observed that only if Yeshua had made medicine on the Sabbath would healing have been forbidden. Yeshua, however, made no medicine on the Sabbath. Again, let us note Yeshua's presence in the synagogue on the Sabbath, worshipping with local Jews according to local custom.

Verses 15–16 portray Yeshua's teaching on proper Sabbath observance. On this occasion, he again used the rabbinic *kal vachomer* style of argumentation in stating:

> "You hypocrites! Each one of you on *Shabbat*—don't you unloose your ox or your donkey from the stall and lead him off to drink? This woman is a daughter of Avraham, and the Adversary kept her tied up for eighteen years. Shouldn't she be freed from this bondage on *Shabbat*?"

The reaction of the Jewish worshippers was one of joy and delight at the Sabbath healings of Yeshua. "But the rest of the crowd were happy about all the wonderful things that were taking place through him [Yeshua]" (v. 17). The common Jewish citizens embraced Yeshua's actions and teachings. This should not surprise us. The people wanted to be met by a God of grace and mercy on the Sabbath. This is precisely what they encountered in Yeshua.

My conclusion from this section of Luke is that Yeshua did end up arguing with some authorities that were in the synagogue. He was found keeping the Sabbath, however, and his arguments concerned *how* to properly keep the Sabbath, not *if* the Sabbath should be kept. His teaching was that of a concerned, compassionate rabbi. Yeshua did indeed transgress the synagogue ruler's understanding of what it meant to observe the Sabbath. However, this was a typical rabbinical halakhic argument, which occurred all the time in Israel. The argument should not affect our view of Yeshua's zealousness to observe the Sabbath. Yeshua contested the synagogue ruler's interpretation of how to observe the Sabbath, a ruler most likely from the school of thought founded by Rabbi Shammai.

In John 5:1–16, Yeshua healed a crippled man on the Sabbath. This occurred at the *Beyt Zata* pool by the Sheep Gate in Jerusalem. There was a particularly negative reaction to this Sabbath healing by an unidentified group of Judean religious authorities (see vv. 10, 16). Problems have arisen from oversimplifying this text, and it is wrongly believed that this opposition was on behalf of the entire Jewish people. This recorded opposition was from a particular group of religious leaders. Possibilities as to their identification include a specific wing of pro-Shammai Pharisees, or certain Sadducean priests, or a mixture of both. The early portion of this text indicates that the point of contention was not necessarily that Yeshua healed on the Sabbath. The problem was that because of his healing, the once crippled man broke some group's understanding of the *avot*[18] of the Sabbath by carrying his rug or mattress. As Fischer noted, "Because He [Yeshua] might depart from some of the competing or varying traditions they departed from God's purpose in the Law."[19]

Safrai observed that even here, Yeshua broke none of the written Torah. In a closed place such as this particular site, one could pick up a mattress and walk without actually transgressing the Torah. Not everyone would do so, but it was not a transgression of the Torah.[20] Vermes said, "In sum, whether in the domain of the Sabbath laws or in that of dietary regulations, it cannot be maintained that Jesus opposed their observance."[21]

Yeshua, then, was fiercely battling here for the correct observance of the Sabbath. It is in this light that we must see all of his arguing regarding the Sabbath.

In conclusion, the evidence shows that Yeshua fervently contended for the Sabbath to be observed correctly. In his teaching and practice of the Sabbath, he strove for an understanding of the correct priorities. He observed the Sabbath with the same desire to fulfill this *mitzvah* as any religious leader of his time. In short, Yeshua's attitude toward keeping the Sabbath reflects his attitude toward the Torah—one of respect and reverence with a passion to fulfill it. This is entirely consistent with what he taught in Matthew 5:17–18, to which I refer the reader.

CHAPTER THREE

YESHUA AND THE KOSHER DIETARY LAWS

Yeshua's Torah observance is also shown in his relationship to the kosher dietary regulations of the Torah. Although there is no teaching of his that is entirely devoted to expounding on the Torah's dietary proscriptions, there is evidence of his practice in this matter.

First, why is it important to single out the kosher dietary *mitzvot* and to observe Yeshua's relationship to them? Throughout the past 3,000 plus years, the Jewish people have looked at כשרות (*kashrut*) as a crucial part of Torah observance. If Yeshua kept the Torah, it would be evidenced by his diet. Leviticus 11 denotes the types of animals and sea creatures the Jewish people were allowed to eat; conversely, it lists the types of animals and sea creatures that were disallowed. By looking at this chapter of the Torah, one sees that any split-hoof, cud-chewing mammal was allowed for food, and that any scaled and finned water creature could be eaten. Other animals, such as rabbits, pigs, and camels are prohibited in this section of the Torah. The chapter concludes with these words:

> For I am the LORD your God. Consecrate yourselves therefore, and be holy, for I am holy. . . . Make a distinction between the unclean and the clean [kosher and non-kosher animals], and between the edible creature and the creature which is not to be eaten. (vv. 44, 47 NASB)

The Torah concept of *holy* is encompassed in the Hebrew word קדוש (*kadosh*), which is used in this Torah portion. It connotes a separation between things set aside for God and things set aside for other purposes. By means of the dietary *mitzvot*, God was separating the Jewish people from the other nations for his special purposes. The dietary laws were part of God's call of separation to the Jewish people. We would then expect that Yeshua, as part of the Jewish people and the nation of Israel, would respect and keep the kosher dietary proscriptions along with the rest of the Torah. Yeshua's teaching, as reflected in the previously mentioned text of Matthew 5:17–18, confirms this.

When we do encounter Yeshua eating, we read of him treating only kosher foods as food. In his actions, and even in his teachings and stories, food consisted of grains, breads, seeds, fruit, and fish. His teachings and stories do not provide a total list of what he would have considered food, but they do give some insight into what he considered acceptable. Let us examine a few incidences.

In Mark 11:12–13, Yeshua became hungry, and went to a fig tree to get some fruit. This demonstrates that Yeshua considered this particular fruit, a staple in first-century Israel, food. As a fruit, it was considered kosher.

In Luke 7:36, Yeshua is asked to dine with a Pharisee, "Now one of the Pharisees was requesting Him to dine with him, and He entered the Pharisee's house and reclined at the table" (NASB). Although this is all the information we learn from the text, again, we can accurately surmise that a Pharisee would only serve his guest kosher food. It is also accurate to assume that if this Pharisee knew that Yeshua did not keep a kosher diet, he would balk at the idea of inviting him to a meal in his house, since proper dietary rituals were an important part of Pharisaic practice.

Luke 22:7–38 records Yeshua and his students celebrating the Passover meal. The foods that were consumed are not specifically mentioned—except for the ritual Passover *matzah* (unleavened bread) and wine. However, we can surmise what they ate from our knowledge of first-century Passover meals. These would have included fruits (such as dates and figs), nuts, *matzah*, wine, a variety of vegetables, lentils, and some type of meat, often lamb. At least, all of the food would have been kosher.

John 6:5–13 records an occasion when Yeshua multiplied the available food. Part of that text reads:

> "There is a lad here who has five barley loaves and two fish. . . ."
> [Yeshua] then took the loaves, and having given thanks, He distributed [the bread] to those who were seated; likewise also of the fish as much as they wanted. (vv. 9, 11 NASB)

Here, Yeshua passed out food to the people he was teaching. The food consisted of bread and fish. It is not stated in the text, but we can surmise that the young man of verse 9 was Jewish, and therefore any fish in his possession would have been kosher. Yeshua fed the group of listeners with kosher fish and bread.

A similar incident occurred in Mark 8:1–9, where again, Yeshua multiplied the available food to feed his listeners. The text records that bread and fish were the foods consumed by everyone present:

> And He directed the people to sit down on the ground; and taking the seven loaves, He gave thanks and broke them, and started giving them to His disciples. . . . They also had a few small fish; and after He had blessed them, He ordered these to be served as well. (vv. 6–7 NASB)

We can conclude that the bread and fish used were consistent with his practice, and thus were kosher.

> When they stepped ashore, they [Simon, Thomas, Nathaniel, James, John] saw a fire of burning coals with a fish on it, and some bread. . . . Yeshua said to them, "Come and have breakfast." None of the *talmidim* dared to ask him, "Who are you?" They knew it was the Lord. Yeshua came, took the bread and gave it to them, and did the same with the fish. (John 21:9, 12–13)

These verses record that Yeshua and some of his closest students ate a meal together on the shore of the Sea of Galilee. In this incident, Yeshua prepared a meal for his students. It is totally logical to expect that he prepared kosher fish, and we note that the food consisted of fish and bread. Mendel Nun, in his work *The Sea of Galilee and Its Fishermen in the New Testament*, identified the types of fish that were caught in the Sea of Galilee during New Testament times, which is where John 21:9–13 takes place. Nun identified both kosher and non-kosher fish. Among the kosher fish are five species of the *amnon* (Hebrew, אמנון, popularly known as St. Peter's Fish), three species of the carp family, and sardines, all popular food in ancient times, and all kosher. In keeping with his observance of the Torah, Yeshua would have prepared kosher fish for the meal described in John 21.

In a number of other instances, Yeshua used food to illustrate his points. It is relevant for us to notice what he considered food.

> Again, the kingdom of heaven is like a dragnet cast into the sea [the Kinneret, or the Sea of Galilee], and gathering fish of every kind; and when it was filled, they drew it up on the beach; and they sat down and gathered the good fish into containers, but the bad they threw away. So it will be at the end of the age; the angels will come forth and take out the wicked from among the righteous. (Matt. 13:47–49)

In this teaching illustration, why would fishermen throw away some of the fish from their catch? Logically, they would do so if the fish were too small, or somehow diseased. Clearly, most of the fish that were thrown away were those that were non-kosher (they did not meet the requirements of the Leviticus 11 list because they did not have fins and scales). The people from Galilee understood this illustration very well. They were familiar with the various types of fish that were caught daily in the Sea of Galilee. Some were kosher; some were not. In this teaching, people are likened to the fish. Some will be kosher (fit) for the kingdom of God, just as some fish are fit for consumption; some will be non-kosher for the kingdom of God, just as some fish are not fit for consumption. By using this illustration, it is evident that Yeshua understood and respected the kosher dietary laws. Otherwise, he would not have used them as a tool for teaching about the kingdom of God.

> "Or what man is there among you who, when his son asks for a loaf, will give him a stone? Or if he asks for a fish, he will not give him a snake, will he?" (Matt. 7:9–10 NASB)

Yeshua and his first century Jewish audience considered a loaf of bread and a fish to be typical foods. The fish would have been kosher (according to Leviticus 11) and the bread would not have contained any non-kosher ingredients. Yeshua refers to bread in at least two other teaching illustrations. He instructed his students on how to pray effectively and acceptably to God: "Give us this day our daily bread" (Matt. 6:11).

Although one could argue for bread being symbolic of the general category of food, it is the food item that Yeshua chose to request from God. Using bread as his food item is consistent with the use of bread as a main staple in the ancient Middle East. In teaching his students to pray in this manner, Yeshua echoed Proverbs 30:8, "Feed me with the food that is my portion" (NASB).

The primary example of Yeshua's using bread to represent food was when he taught his students to ask God to provide food for them on a daily basis. This illustrated the reality that bread was an important daily food item.

Yeshua's Teachings and *Kashrut*

Yeshua's teachings have sometimes been misunderstood so as to cast doubt on the validity of *kashrut*. For example, Yeshua's teaching in Matthew 15:11–20 is often misunderstood regarding this issue.

"It is not what enters into the mouth that defiles the man, but what proceeds out of the mouth, this defiles the man. . . . Everything that goes into the mouth passes into the stomach, and is eliminated. . . . But the things that proceed out of the mouth come from the heart, and those defile the man. For out of the heart come evil thoughts, murders, adulteries, fornications, thefts, false witness, slanders. These are the things which defile the man; but to eat with unwashed hands does not defile the man." (NASB)

In this passage, Yeshua nowhere negated the validity of *kashrut*. To do so would contradict his statement of Matthew 5:17–18, where he said he had not come to abolish the Law. Instead, Yeshua was teaching about the misconceptions of the נטילת ידיים (Hebrew, *n'tilat yadayim*, the ritual hand washing before meals). The group of Pharisees in this text always carried out this ritual hand washing before each meal, believing that not to do so according to their specific method would cause a person to be ritually defiled. Therefore, Yeshua said, "To eat with unwashed hands does not defile the man." That is, not performing the ritual hand-washing ceremony according to the method of this group of first-century Pharisees did not make one impure before God, and thereby did not obligate the person to cleanse himself ritually. Matthew 15:1–2 describes the context of this incident:

Then some Pharisees and scribes came to Jesus from Jerusalem and said, "Why do your disciples break the traditions of the elders? For they do not wash their hands when they eat bread." (NASB)

The exact identification of this group of Pharisees and scribes is difficult to determine. However, they scrupulously practiced the *n'tilat yadayim* ritual before eating (much as Orthodox Jewry does today). Apparently, as today, this was not a universally practiced custom. At least we see that it was not so widespread among Galilean Jews. In Matthew 15:2, it is considered a type of "tradition of the elders." In the Greek text παραδοσιν των πρεσβυτερων (*paradosin ton presbuteron*) reflects the Hebrew concept מסורתי האבות (*masortey ha'avot*, or "traditions of the fathers") and not a mandated *mitzvah* from the Torah. This concept denotes the development of traditions, not necessarily found in the Torah, which deal with how to perform a certain *mitzvah*. (Blessing God for food, however, can indeed be considered a Torah-mandated *mitzvah*).

This group accused Yeshua of breaking the Pharisaic tradition of *n'tilat yadayim* and questioned his connection to the above mentioned *masortey ha'avot.* They believed that Yeshua taught his students incorrectly, since he did not teach them to fulfill the *mitzvot* in the same manner as their wing of Pharisaic teachers did. This reflects the fact that Yeshua did not accept the authority of these particular Pharisees' traditions (or *masoret ha'avot*). This fact, in itself, caused political problems with this branch of Pharisaism. Yeshua discoursed with these accusers and charged them with a far greater oversight. In the end, he taught his students that foods and their accompanying rituals do not make a person clean or unclean before God. Instead, he challenged his students to see that the thoughts and intents of their hearts make one clean or unclean before God. Before we conclude, according to this teaching, that *kashrut* is no longer valid, let us understand what Yeshua would have regarded as food. Yeshua, who honored and practiced Torah, would have considered the list in Leviticus 11 to be the appropriate designation of proper and improper foods.

We need to determine what Yeshua was referring to in Matthew 15:11. In order *not* to defile a first-century Jew, the food would have had to be kosher according to the definition of Leviticus 11. If a Jewish person ate non-kosher food, it *would* have defiled him (also see Matt. 15:19). To sum up, Yeshua was teaching that when a Jewish person ate kosher food and did not perform the *n'tilat yadayim* ceremony beforehand, he was not defiled. He then proceeded to show what did defile a man. This teaching in no way denies the validity of *kashrut*, and in fact supports it as part of the Torah—*if* we understand food as being limited to the Leviticus 11 definition. This is the understanding that Yeshua would have had.

In *The Jewish People in the First Century*,[1] Safrai and Stern have provided us with an understanding of the first-century diet among Jewish communities in the Land of Israel. They list vegetables and fish as fundamental dietary items, along with bread, oil, wine, and sauces, and a variety of fruits as being part of the kosher diet. Lentil soup and dip were also popular food items. Of course, wealthier people would have access to more meat products, while poorer people would eat less meat and more vegetables and grains. Honey and vegetables were cultivated food items in the Land at that time, as well.

The picture we have of Yeshua from the New Testament is one in which he ate the foods mentioned above. All of them would have been considered kosher.

Conclusion

Yeshua kept a kosher diet. There is no particular emphasis on this in the New Testament because, at the time of its writing, it was a non-issue. We can determine Yeshua's dietary practices by paying attention to the use of food in the Gospel narratives. Every individual in Israel's Jewish communities normally maintained a kosher diet, which was defined by Leviticus 11. There is not one instance in the Gospels of Yeshua eating food that is not kosher. The things that we do see him eating and drinking (bread, fish, fruits, water, and wine) were kosher staples of first-century Israel. In fact, Israel was known for having seven species of produce that were abundant in the Land: dates, figs, olives, wheat, barley, grapes, and pomegranates. Since there is no sure proof, we can surmise that Yeshua (along with the rest of the Jewish people of that period) ate these species. In Matthew 8:28–34, the one time when Yeshua encountered swine (which are non-kosher animals), he gave no indication that he considered them to be food.

Finally, let us remember that Yeshua's dietary practices would have been in keeping with his teaching. Again, I refer the reader to Matthew 5:17–18, where Yeshua's words argue for a kosher diet, as designated in the Torah.

Yeshua's dietary practices also confirm his Torah observance. Again, there is no major emphasis on this point in the New Testament because it was a non-issue. It was not a factor in recording the historical narratives of Yeshua's life because all of first-century Israel would have known (and even taken for granted) the fact that Yeshua kept a kosher diet, as did every normal Jewish citizen in first-century Israel.

CHAPTER FOUR

OTHER EXAMPLES OF YESHUA'S TORAH OBSERVANCE

In this chapter on Yeshua's Torah observance, we will look at Scriptures from Matthew, Mark, Luke, and John that testify to Yeshua's Torah-observant lifestyle. We will see that the four narrative recorders agree on the approach that Yeshua took toward the Torah. This chapter is arranged in the order of the Gospel narratives.

Matthew and John spent good portions of their lives with Yeshua as part of his inner circle of students. Therefore, their narratives and proofs are especially meaningful for us. In addition, Luke and Mark also belonged to the first generation of Messianic Jews, and therefore, were very closely tied to the people, events, and teachings of Yeshua's life. Their historical narratives are invaluable for us as sources to show Yeshua's Torah observance.

This chapter is not an exhaustive study of the matter, but rather, it identifies some of the Scriptures that furnish proof of Yeshua's attitude toward the Torah. In addition, it is hoped that the reader will find more proofs in his/her own study of the four historical narratives of Yeshua's life.

The following table will refer the reader to portions of the book of Matthew, as well as show the various *mitzvot* that Yeshua fulfilled.

Yeshua's Torah Observance in the Book of Matthew

The Scripture	The Mitzvah
5:17–18	Yeshua teaches that the Torah retains its validity until planet earth passes away.
7:12	The Torah is the basis of Yeshua's teachings.
8:1–4	Yeshua commands a healed Jewish man to fulfill a sacrificial *mitzvah* (see Lev. 13 and 14).

Yeshua's Torah Observance in the Book of Matthew *(cont.)*

The Scripture   *The Mitzvah*

8:19   A Torah teacher would only be willing to be Yeshua's disciple if Yeshua was Torah-observant.

19:16–19   Yeshua encouraged a Torah-observant man to keep the *mitzvot*.

Matthew gave strong evidence that Yeshua was Torah-observant. Though he differed with some of his contemporary religious authorities on how to keep various *mitzvot* of the Torah, the issue of observance, as a way of life, is not contested in the Gospels. I agree with the Jewish scholar Geza Vermes, who noted, "Did Jesus reject these [the Mosaic Laws]? The Synoptic Gospels, our primary witnesses, give no support to such a theory."[1]

In summing up his view of Yeshua in the Gospels, Vermes observed, "The only logical inference is that Jesus freely insisted, even in a purely ritual context, on strict adherence to the Torah."[2]

Yeshua's Teaching Regarding the Role of the Torah

Yeshua's teaching on the role of the Torah needs to be mentioned here, and the book of Matthew has a lot to tell us about this subject. An understanding of this will give us more of a complete picture of Yeshua's life and teachings. My colleagues, Ariel and D'vorah Berkowitz, have accurately summarized the teachings of Yeshua on the Torah in their book *Torah Rediscovered*. Therefore, I will not give a long discourse on Yeshua's teachings, as I am in full agreement with their explanations on this matter. Two separate teachings of Yeshua on the Torah, however, have so profoundly struck me over the past few years that they bear mentioning here.

First, Matthew 5:17–19 is a powerful teaching that cannot be ignored by any serious student of the Torah-New Testament relationship. In fact, it may be considered an אב (*av*)[3] in understanding Yeshua's attitude toward the Torah, if I may borrow this category from rabbinic thought. Yeshua clearly taught on the time span of the Torah's validity:

> Don't think that I have come to abolish the *Torah* or the Prophets. I have come not to abolish but to complete. Yes, indeed! I tell you that until heaven and earth pass away, not so much as a *yud* or a stroke will pass from the *Torah*—not until everything that must happen has happened. (5:17–18)

The Messiah taught that his influence would be one of strengthening, not weakening, the Torah. The Greek word used in the text for *complete* is πλϵρωσαι (*plerosai*). It carries a sense of both fulfilling and establishing the proper meaning of the Torah. Israeli scholar David Bivin has accurately paraphrased the meaning of Yeshua's words in rendering the passage as follows:

> Never imagine for a moment, Jesus says, that I intend to abrogate the Law by misinterpreting it. My intent is not to weaken or negate the Law, but by properly interpreting God's Written Word I aim to establish it, that is, make it even more lasting. I would never invalidate the Law by . . . removing something from it through misinterpretation. Heaven and earth would sooner disappear than something from the Law. Not the smallest letter in the alphabet, the *yod*, nor even its decorative spur, will ever disappear from the Law.[4]

Yeshua was teaching that he had profound respect for the Law, that is, the Torah. The Greek word often translated in this verse as Law is νομον, *nomon*, and without a doubt, it means the Torah. Therefore, we must see all of Yeshua's teachings and actions, as well as those of his students, as being consistent with his teaching in Matthew 5. The foundation that has been laid is one of love and respect for the Torah. As Fischer noted:

> Matthew 5:17–19 is the crucial passage in understanding Jesus' perspective. In it he uses the term "fulfill" [*plerosai*] to describe his relationship to the Law . . . here it implies to cram full, bring to full expression, show forth the intended meaning. The idea is to give fulness and provide true meaning, as opposed to destroying, overthrowing or abolishing.[5]

The best educated guess for the Hebrew word Yeshua spoke here for *fulfill* is לקיים (*l'kayyem*). In its vernacular and rabbinic usage at that time, *l'kayyem* connoted to teach correctly regarding a subject. Fischer was therefore correct when he said, "The idea is to . . . provide true meaning."

In addition, Matthew 24:12 holds profound significance for us. In this verse, Yeshua was teaching on the signs of the end of the age (the Hebrew concept of אחרית הימים, *acharit hayamim*).[6] The NIV translates this verse as: "Because of the increase of wickedness, the love of most will grow cold." The *Complete Jewish Bible* does more justice to the verse: "Many people's love will grow cold because of increased distance from *Torah*." The Greek text states:

και δια το πληθυνθηναι την ανομιαν ψυγησϵται η αγαπη των πολλων (*kai dia to plethunthenai ten anomian psugesetai he agape ton pollon*).

This literally refers to the growth of lawlessness as causing the love of one's brother to die down as a social norm in the last days. The word *anomian* is what captures our attention here. It literally means "without law, or Torah." It is rightly translated "distance from the Torah." The lawlessness being referred to here is best understood in its biblical and Jewish context. When Yeshua talked about *Law*, there was only one Law to which he was referring, and that is the Torah. The *Complete Jewish Bible* captures the essence of Yeshua's point, which is that the world as a whole will be moving away from the ideals of the Torah as set down in the Scriptures. This will cause cruelty to abound on an international scale. We see examples of this in the modern world, and in societal breakdown in many cultures, where violent crime and sexual immorality (two issues addressed by the Torah) are rampant.

What does this teach us regarding Yeshua's attitude toward the Torah? The obvious answer is that Yeshua greatly respected it, stating that the world situation in the *acharit hayamim* will deteriorate because people will not respect the Torah or its teachings.

These two sections of Scripture (Matthew 5 and 24) give us a consistent picture of the teaching of Yeshua regarding the Torah. His message is that the Torah is valid and is to be respected and observed. In fact, such a conclusion is held by a growing number of Jewish and Christian scholars. In his work *Jesus and Early Judaism*, Dr. Fischer noted eight outstanding scholars who believe in the Torah observance of Yeshua. These include Jewish scholars David Flusser, Jules Isaac, Shmuel Safrai, and Pinchas Lapide; Christian scholars Robert Lindsey, David Bivin, and Brad Young assert the same. It is heartening to note that in our day, both Jewish and Christian scholars clearly see that Yeshua observed the Torah.

We can also see Yeshua's respect for and adherence to the Torah in Luke 24. For example, in verse 27, Yeshua was walking with some of his students after he rose from the dead: "Then starting with Moshe [Moses] and all the prophets, he explained to them the things that can be found throughout the *Tanakh* concerning himself." In Luke 24:44, Yeshua was in Jerusalem with his students when he said, "When I was still with you . . . [I] told you that everything written about me in the *Torah* of Moshe, the Prophets and the Psalms had to be fulfilled."

In both of these occasions, using the Torah, Yeshua explained to his students what had to happen to him. In verse 44, he made the point that the Torah was a correct source for knowing about the Messiah. This tells us something about his attitude toward the Torah, does it not? Certainly, if Yeshua were not Torah-observant or respectful towards the Torah, he would not have said what he did.

Another example is found in Matthew 7:12, where Yeshua gave a summary teaching of the message of the Scriptures: "Always treat others as you would like them to treat you; that sums up the teaching of the *Torah* and the Prophets." The words of the Torah and the Prophets were the source of Yeshua's main teachings. Many people have brought out the similarity between this teaching and that of Rabbi Hillel, who, in his prime, was a generation before Yeshua. Hillel taught, "What is hateful to you, do not do to your fellow. That is the whole Torah; the rest is commentary—go and study" (*Shabbat* 31a). It is easily surmised that both Yeshua and Hillel, in their summary teachings, were commenting upon Leviticus 19:18 (which Yeshua mentioned in another New Testament text as one of the two most important *mitzvot*). No one doubts Hillel's Torah-observant lifestyle. There is no difference between Hillel's source and Yeshua's source regarding their similar teaching here. Hillel was commenting on the Torah, and Yeshua was commenting on the Torah. This tells us that they both greatly respected the Torah. It was the source for their summary statements on behavior.

To sum up, Matthew presents us with teachings of Yeshua that demonstrate his Torah observance, as well as his great respect for the Torah.

Yeshua's Torah Observance in the Book of Mark

We have previously seen in the book of Mark how Yeshua observed the Sabbath (see 1:21; 3:1–6; 6:1–2) and upheld the Torah's ritual cleansing *mitzvot* (see 1:44). In Mark 1:39 we read: "So he traveled all through the Galil [Galilee], preaching in their synagogues and expelling demons."

The Healer

Mark 1:39 would be a doubtful scenario if Yeshua were not Torah-observant. He would not have been received into a group of Galilean synagogues in the role of a rabbi and a healer if he were not Torah-observant, at least by Galilean standards. As Lee pointed out in his work, this was most certainly the case.[7] In Mark 5:21–43, we have a relevant scenario in which to see Yeshua's attitude toward the Torah. Jairus, as the head official of his synagogue (see v. 22) approached Yeshua in his role as rabbi and healer and begged him to heal his daughter (see v. 23). Yeshua was given the right as rabbi and healer to enter Jairus' house (see vv. 38–39). Yeshua was accepted in his role as a rabbi by a leading synagogue official who was Torah-observant himself. It is reasonable to assume that Jairus would not have asked Yeshua for help if Yeshua were not also Torah-observant, in spite of the fact that Jairus had a desperate need.

Honoring Parents

In Mark 7:10–13, Yeshua showed his respect for the Torah when he stated, "Moshe said, 'Honor your father and your mother,' and 'Anyone who curses his father or mother must be put to death.'" These are direct quotes from the Torah: "Honor your father and mother so that you may live long in the land which ADONAI your God is giving you" (Ex. 20:12; see also Deut. 5:16). Yeshua also quoted Exodus 21:17: "Whoever curses his father or mother must be put to death."

Yeshua used these verses to reprove certain Pharisees and teachers who, through their interpretation of Scripture, negated the *mitzvot* of honoring one's parents. Yeshua referred to the above verses as the final, authoritative principles upon which children should relate to their parents. By doing this, he clearly showed his great respect for the Torah.

Yeshua's Torah Observance in the Book of Luke

A Glimpse Through Luke's Eyes

Dr. Fischer, of Netzer David Yeshiva, suggests the possibility that Luke was a relative of Paul and a Torah-observant Jew himself. If so, we have a new set of eyes with which to view this Gospel narrative. Although all scholars do not agree on this point, I sympathize with Fischer and will work from the premise that Luke was either a Torah-observant Jew or a Torah-observant Godfearer. (See "Torah Observance in Philippi" in chapter 5, for a full explanation of the term *Godfearer*.) Dr. David Flusser also suggested that Theophilus, the recipient of Luke and Acts, was a member of the High Priest's family. If so, we can see Luke's writings with renewed eyes.[8]

For example, Luke 1 makes it very clear that John the Baptist's family, of priestly heritage, was strictly Torah-observant. If Flusser's idea that Theophilus was a high-ranking priest is correct, Theophilus would have been favorably impressed if there was a strong connection between Yeshua and the Temple ritual. In addition, Theophilus would most likely have been a Sadducee. To a Sadducee, the Temple rituals, carried out by the priests, were the backbone of true Judaism. Although Yeshua himself did not belong to the Aaronic priesthood, his family had priestly ties in it through John's branch of the family. In fact, John himself was a priest. Certain other priests may have looked upon the fact that John, a priest, supported Yeshua's claim to Messiahship, with some favor. To a twentieth-century Western reader, this may seem like an irrelevant fact, not worthy of emphasis, but in the first-century world of Israel, establishing noteworthy family ties was very important. One's reputation and ability to be accepted by others (especially in the religious hierarchy in Jerusalem) was linked to family genealogy. The picture (Luke 2) of the humble Torah observance of Yeshua's immediate family would also have made a positive impression upon Theophilus. At the very least, Theophilus would have had no grounds on which to doubt the good lineage and Torah observance of this extended family. In today's world, such a family lineage may not count for much, but in the world of first-century Israeli Judaism, it was one of the most important aspects in proving one's character, honor, reputation, and social standing. Let us not discount the power of the picture painted in the first two chapters of Luke concerning Yeshua's family. A Torah-observant background is there for us to see.

Let us now examine some important examples of Yeshua's Torah observance. Then, we will conclude our sketch of Luke's evidence by providing the particular observance with its corresponding reference in the Torah.

His Relationship with the Torah

Shortly after these events in the book of Luke, we again see the great respect with which Yeshua held the Scriptures of the Torah. In Luke 4:1–13, Yeshua was tempted with difficult trials. In each matter, he dealt with the temptation by quoting from the Torah (Deut. 8:3; 6:13–14; Ps. 91:11–12). These verses represent the truth, and they became Yeshua's spiritual, emotional, and psychological defense against the evil he faced. Notice that the first two Scriptures come from the Torah. Words from the Torah sustained Yeshua at this time of need. This helps us see how important the Torah and its truths were in his life. This incident in Luke's narrative gives more power to Rabbi Falk's statement, quoted previously, that "He [Yeshua] strengthened the Torah of Moses majestically . . . not one of our sages spoke out more emphatically concerning the immutability of the Torah."[9]

As an adult, Yeshua continued in the Torah-observant ways of his youth: "He taught in their synagogues, and everyone respected him" (Luke 4:15). Yeshua continued to worship and take part in the Torah-centered education of the local synagogues. According to this verse, he was well respected by the public as a teacher (rabbi). This could only be possible if he continued to be Torah-observant. Luke 4:16 confirms his continual participation as an adult in synagogue worship and learning— "On *Shabbat* he went to the synagogue as usual."

Here, we see that Yeshua's participation in local synagogue worship and custom was his usual activity. Yeshua was educated in the Torah in his local synagogue. As every Galilean Jew, Yeshua learned the Torah—how to read it, memorize it, and its principles and customs, from both his family and his local synagogue. It was part of his life as a Jew.

In 4:16b–17, Yeshua is shown as taking an active part in a Sabbath worship service. He was given the traditional role as שליח ציבור (*shaliach tzibbur*).[10] He read the section from the Prophets and expounded on the verses, a role reserved in his day for a rabbi or rabbi in training. His participation should be seen as a normal Galilean Jewish expression of worship to God. Here, the description of Yeshua fits the normal lifestyle of a Torah-observant teacher of his era. In Luke 4:31, Yeshua continued with his Torah teaching in the village of Capernaum. There, too, he took part in normal Sabbath worship and ritual: "He went down to K'far-Nachum (Capernaum) . . . and made a practice of teaching them on *Shabbat*."

Dealing with a Skin Disease

In his role as a rabbi and healer, Yeshua was careful to keep the *mitzvot* of the Torah and to instruct his students and kinsmen to do the same. An example of this is found in Luke 5:12–16 where Yeshua healed a Jewish leper.

> Immediately the *tzara'at* [skin disease] left him. Then Yeshua warned him not to tell anyone. "Instead, as a testimony to the people, go straight to the *cohen* [priest] and make an offering for your cleansing, as Moshe commanded."

Here, Yeshua healed a sick man and instructed him to offer the sacrifice given in the Torah for such a healing, as well as to be pronounced healed by the priest on duty, according to Leviticus 14:1–32. Yeshua was instructing his healed kinsman to keep the *mitzvah* of the Torah.

> "This is to be the law concerning the person afflicted with *tzara'at* on the day of his purification. He is to be brought to the *cohen* [priest]. . . . If he [the *cohen*] sees that the *tzara'at* sores have been healed . . . then the *cohen* will order that two living clean birds be taken for the one to be purified, along with cedar-wood, scarlet yarn and oregano leaves. . . . He who is to be purified must wash his clothes, shave off all his hair and bathe himself in water. Then he will be clean; and after that, he may enter the camp; but he must

live outside his tent for seven days. . . . On the eighth day he is to take two male lambs without defect, one female lamb in its first year without defect and six-and-a-half quarts of fine flour for a grain offering, mixed with olive oil, and two-thirds of a pint of olive oil. (Lev. 14:2–4, 8, 10)

Yeshua was instructing this man to report to a priest, be examined and pronounced healed, make an immediate offering, be quarantined for a week, and then offer the final sacrifice. Yeshua upheld these *mitzvot* of the Torah. His actions and instructions were in line with a Torah-observant lifestyle.

Fulfilling the Mitzvah of Tzitzit

When sick people approached Yeshua for healing, they tried to touch the fringes (Hebrew, צִיצִת, *tzitzit*) on his clothes. The fringes were attached to the garments of every Jewish male in accordance with the *mitzvah* found in Numbers 15:37–41: "Make . . . *tzitziyot* [plural] on the corners of [their garments], and . . . put with the *tzitzit* on each corner a blue thread."

By wearing the fringes on his clothes, Yeshua was directly fulfilling a *mitzvah* from the Torah. The Israeli scholar Shmuel Safrai noted, "I suppose that he [Yeshua] and his students used both of them [*tzitzit* and *t'fillin*]."[11]

In Luke 8:43–48, Yeshua is approached by an ill woman who grabbed the "fringe of His cloak" (NASB), thereby seizing his *tzitzit*, also. We are not told whether this was an incidental or purposeful grabbing of the *tzitzit*. (In more modern times, it has become a custom for a few groups to touch a sage's *tzitzit* as a sign of great respect.) However, what is relevant is the fact that Yeshua wore the fringes of Numbers 15, and Luke gives us a picture of that here.

There are additional examples of Yeshua teaching other Jews to keep the 613 *mitzvot* of the Torah. In Luke 18:18–30, a wealthy leader approached Yeshua and asked, "Good rabbi, what should I do to obtain eternal life?" (v. 18). Yeshua, not surprisingly, cited certain *mitzvot* from Exodus 20: "You know the *mitzvot*—Don't commit adultery, don't murder, don't steal, don't give false testimony, honor your father and mother" (v. 20). Yeshua reviewed what the man already knew and practiced—the *mitzvot* of the Torah. This is clear from the man's reply: "I have kept all these since I was a boy" (v. 21).

In this passage, Yeshua upheld the sanctity of the *mitzvot* in the Torah. Seeing the condition of the man's personal life, however, he added a stipulation that could have caused the man to dedicate his life more fully to God. While upholding the place and authority of the Torah, Yeshua explained to the man how to establish the Torah (i.e., how to fulfill the *mitzvot* of Deuteronomy 6:4 and Leviticus 19:18).[12] The point is that Yeshua upheld the importance of fulfilling the *mitzvot*, while applying an accepted and Torah-observant teaching to this situation.

The following table from Luke's narrative shows Yeshua's Torah observance and the *mitzvah* he was keeping.

Yeshua's Torah Observance and Keeping of Mitzvot

Luke	The Mitzvah
8:44	Yeshua wore fringes according to Numbers 15:37 ff.
9:16	Yeshua blessed food according to Exodus 23:25.
10:25–28	Yeshua encouraged a Torah-teacher to keep Deuteronomy 6:4 and Leviticus 19:18.
11:27–28	Yeshua taught that they who keep the "word," which includes the Torah and its *mitzvot*, are blessed.
16:16–17	Yeshua taught that the Torah will not pass away until physical planet earth passes away.
17:11–15	Yeshua encouraged receivers of God's mercy to obey Torah by carrying out the *mitzvot* pertaining to skin diseases.
18:18–24	Yeshua encouraged a man to observe the Exodus 20 *mitzvot*.
19:28 ff.	Yeshua arrived in Jerusalem, fulfilling Exodus 23:17.
22:14–20	Yeshua recited the story of Passover and kept the festival (see Exod. 13:14–16).
23:56	Yeshua's students kept the Sabbath, even on such a tension-filled day, thereby reflecting their rabbi's attitude toward the Sabbath.

These verses describe Yeshua's devotion to the Torah. My conclusion, then, is that the gospel of Luke also confirms Yeshua's Torah-observant lifestyle. This is particularly significant in that there has been a historical, theological stereotype that Luke is the most Gentile of all Gospel writers in his tone, narrative, and picture of Yeshua. The evidence, however, does not support this stereotype. In fact, it does quite the opposite.

Yeshua's Torah Observance in the Book of John

The book written by *Yochanan ben Zavdai* (John, son of Zebedee), one of Yeshua's closest friends, also attests to Yeshua's Torah observance. We will look at four fascinating examples of such observance.

The Rabbi

In John 3:1, Nicodemus, a Pharisee and rabbi, approached Yeshua and called him "rabbi." Only a Torah-observant Jew who was well educated and/or ordained merited this title, especially in the world of the Pharisees. The title *rabbi*, in first-century Israel, attested to a person's role as a recognized teacher (by a particular wing or sect of Judaism). Nicodemus then testified to the fact that he believed Yeshua's miracles to be acts of God.

> This man came to Yeshua by night and said to him, "Rabbi, we know it is from God that you have come as a teacher; for no one can do these miracles you perform unless God is with him." (John 3:2)

Yeshua had to have been a Torah-observant rabbi in order for a Pharisaic rabbi such as Nicodemus to respect him, as the text indicates. Otherwise, the text would not fit the context. The only other possibility is that Nicodemus called Yeshua *rabbi* in mockery, but that is hardly possible because Nicodemus is portrayed as a sincere person. The scribe who wrote the book of John used the Hebrew word *rabbi* in Greek, without trying to find a similar Greek word. The Greek word διδασχαλος (*didaschalos*, teacher), which is sometime used for a rabbi, is not used in the text. This preserves the original Hebrew context and shows us that Yeshua's title portrays him as part of the world of first-century Israeli Judaism. Yeshua was not just Torah-observant; he was a Torah-observant *rabbi*. He was a teacher of the Torah, and was recognized as such by people in his native area.

Later in the book of John, Yeshua is quoted as having defended the honor and position of the Torah. In a discussion with some unidentified Judean leaders, he stated:

> "But don't think that it is I who will be your accuser before the Father. Do you know who will accuse you? Moshe, the very one

you have counted on! For if you really believed Moshe, you
would believe me; because it was about me that he wrote."
(5:45–46)

Yeshua illustrated the great importance of the Mosaic revelation in
God's plan. He stated that the leaders to whom he was speaking ought to
have believed the revelations and prophecies of Moses. Because they did
not, they misunderstood Yeshua's role. Thus, Yeshua again upheld the
truth and relevance of the Torah by emphasizing the importance of
knowing and believing the Torah. Only a Torah-observant Jew would
have said and taught this. He is described here as zealous to uphold the
truth of the Torah's message.

John 6:11 affirms Yeshua's observance:

Then Yeshua took the loaves of bread, and, after making a
b'rakhah [blessing], gave to all who were sitting there, and likewise with the fish, as much as they wanted.

It appears that Yeshua gave the contemporary blessing over a meal
with bread, as it was known to exist at this time.[7] In doing so, he know-
ingly fulfilled a *mitzvah* from the Mosaic Covenant. "But you shall serve
the Lord your God, and He will bless your bread and water; and I will re-
move sickness from your midst" (Exod. 23:25 NASB).

Keeping the Mitzvah of Sukkot

John 7:2 ff. reveals another example of Yeshua's loyalty to the Torah. In
this case, we observe Yeshua participating in one of the pilgrimage festivals, *Sukkot* (Feast of Booths). The text states, "But the festival of *Sukkot*
in Y'hudah [Judah] was near. . . . [Yeshua], too, went up [to Jerusalem],
not publicly but in secret."

By going to Jerusalem, Yeshua was fulfilling the *mitzvah* to observe
Sukkot. This *mitzvah* is commanded to Israel (Lev. 23:33–43; Num.
29:12–39; Deut. 16:13–16; Exod. 23:17). The Exodus version states,
"Three times a year all your men are to appear before the Lord, ADONAI."
The Talmud's description of the pilgrimage parades with the great rejoic-
ing in Jerusalem during first-century *Sukkot* celebrations attests to this
festival's importance.

While he was fulfilling the *Sukkot mitzvah*, Yeshua did a great
amount of teaching in the Temple area. Teaching at festivals was an accepted rabbinic practice, but he did not go up to Jerusalem merely to
teach crowds. The text indicates that he obeyed this *mitzvah* to fulfill the
Torah. In John 7:14–24, Yeshua criticized some Judeans for misjudging

him during his *Sukkot* teaching sessions: "Did not Moshe give you the *Torah*? Yet not one of you obeys the *Torah*!" (v. 19).

Rebuking them, Yeshua implied that these authorities rightly understood the Divine authority and gift that God gave the people through the Torah. Yet, they did not keep the *mitzvot* properly. Clearly, he indicated that the *mitzvot* should be observed; however, they should be kept in the correct manner. This is similar to his statement in Matthew 23:1, "The Torah teachers and the *P'rushim* [Pharisees] . . . sit in the seat of Moshe. So whatever they tell you, take care to do it. But don't do what they do, because they talk but don't act."

Yeshua emphasized that the main ideas of these teachers were to be carried out. Their primary teachings were derived directly from the Torah. He was upholding the authority of the Torah. His objection to these religious authorities (see Matthew 23) was not to their teaching, but to their hypocrisy (vv. 4–7; 27–28); their pompousness (vv. 23: 8–12); their mistreatment of people in general and converts in particular (vv. 13–15); their misinterpretation of some of the *mitzvot* (vv. 16–24); and their pride (vv. 29–32). Earlier in this book, we noted that Yeshua's teaching was an integrated whole—he practiced what he taught. This was not the case with this group of leaders in Matthew 23.

However, Yeshua upheld the source of their teaching and its authority. Again, this demonstrates that his attitude toward the Torah was respectful. He indicated that it was an obligation for the people to observe and fulfill the *mitzvot* of the Torah. Although he had problems with some of the Torah's teachers, he had none with the Torah itself. In fact, he affirmed that it is valid to keep the most detailed and minute agricultural tithing *mitzvot*.

> "You pay your tithes of mint, dill and cumin; but you have neglected the weightier matters of the *Torah*—justice, mercy, trust. These are the things you should have attended to—without neglecting the others!" (Matt. 23:23)

Even in the midst of giving a stern rebuke, Yeshua upheld the validity and truth of the Torah's *mitzvot*—all of them!

Keeping the Mitzvah of Passover

In addition to *Sukkot*, John provides an additional opportunity to see how Yeshua observed another one of Israel's holy days, Passover. By examining Yeshua's observance of Passover, we can again see his positive attitude toward the Torah. The original *mitzvot* on keeping Passover are found in Exodus 12:11–48, Exodus 23:14–15, Numbers 9:2 ff.,

Deuteronomy 16:1 ff., and Leviticus 23:4–6, which reads:

> These are the holy times given by God. . . . In the first month on the fourteenth day in the evening is God's Passover. On the fifteenth day of this month is God's festival of unleavened bread. You will eat unleavened bread for seven days (vv. 4–5, author's translation).

Deuteronomy 16:16 states, "Three times a year all your males shall appear before the Lord your God . . . [this includes] the feast of Unleavened Bread" (NASB). Passover was another pilgrimage festival. It took place in the spring during the month of Nisan. Again, huge numbers of Jewish pilgrims would ascend to Jerusalem to sacrifice, retell the Passover story, and eat the Passover meal (Hebrew, סדר, *seder*). While the New Covenant does not emphasize the matter, it shows that Yeshua fulfilled these Passover *mitzvot*. According to John 2:13, "It was almost time for the festival of *Pesach* [Passover] in Y'hudah [Judah], so Yeshua went up to Yerushalayim [Jerusalem]." Yeshua went up to Jerusalem in order to fulfill the Passover *mitzvot*, as all Israel's men were commanded to do (see Exod. 23:14–15). In John 2:13, Yeshua was fulfilling the Passover *mitzvot*. Again, even if it can be said that he engaged in teaching as his primary activity on the trip to Jerusalem, it is no coincidence that he went there during Passover. He fulfilled the *mitzvot* regarding the festival.

John records additional information about Yeshua and Passover. In John 11:55, we read that it is Passover again, two years after the John 2 narrative. In Jerusalem, the pilgrims are expecting the Galilean rabbi and prophet Yeshua to come and teach them (see v. 56). The ruling Temple priests and some Pharisees also expected Yeshua to come and fulfill the *mitzvot*, as well as teach (see v. 57). This shows that both common people and rabbis expected Yeshua in Jerusalem during Passover. To no one's surprise, he arrived in Jerusalem to fulfill the *mitzvah* and to teach (see 12:12–16).[13]

His Authority

There is one final example of Yeshua's Torah faithfulness that we will examine from John's Gospel. In John 8:12–20, Yeshua was challenged as to the validity of his witness (his teaching and authority): "You're testifying on your own behalf; your testimony [according to Torah] is not valid." This means that some people were accusing Yeshua of having no one else in a place of authority who could back up what he said about himself.

Part of Yeshua's defense was taken directly from the Torah, thus up-holding its importance and truth. Yeshua responded to the charge in 8:13 by saying, "And even in your *Torah* it is written that the testimony of two people is valid. I myself testify on my own behalf, and so does the Father who sent me" (vv. 17–18). Yeshua quoted directly from Deuteronomy 19:15: "On the evidence of two or three witnesses a matter will be confirmed [legally]" (NASB).

Yeshua rested his argument on one of the Torah's *mitzvot*. He made the point that he had two valid witnesses to his authority—his father and himself. The point is that Yeshua used the Torah to argue for his own validity as prophet, teacher, and Messiah.

Conclusion from the Four Historical Narratives

We have seen ample evidence from the four Gospels that Yeshua was a Jewish man who lived his earthly life in absolute loyalty to the sacred covenants that God made with his people, Israel. Yeshua was a Torah-observant Jewish man. By taking the Scripture in a literal-historical sense, this is the only conclusion we can come to. Any other conclusion flies directly in the face of all of the facts. As Fischer noted:

> He [Yeshua] affirmed the important principles of Jewish faith: belief in God the Creator . . . the Jewish people as chosen by God, the Jewish Scriptures as authoritative and divine, reward and punishment from God, resurrection, creation under God's care, and Gehenna.[14]

I will sum up this section with the words of the Israeli scholars Dr. Safrai and Dr. Flusser. Safrai noted, "Yeshua filled up the Law and Jewish traditions of the Second Temple Period."[15] Flusser commented:

> Jesus adhered to the standard Judaism of his time, and from this point of view it is natural that his disciples, and after them the Jewish Christian community, should have lived according to the Law.[16]

This short exploration of the four Gospels upholds Yeshua's Torah observance.

PART TWO

YESHUA'S *TALMIDIM* AND THE TORAH

HOW DID PAUL LIVE?

It is important to establish a link in Torah observance from rabbi to students. We have seen that Yeshua was Torah-observant. Therefore, we should expect to see a Torah-observant lifestyle in the lives of his students. This chapter will focus on Yeshua's most famous follower, Paul of Tarsus, or as I will refer to him, (Rabbi/*Rav*) *Sha'ul*. If my thesis about Yeshua is correct, then *Sha'ul* must replicate the same zeal for Torah observance that his rabbi, Yeshua, had.

Many modern scholars have proven that Rabbi *Sha'ul* lived as a Jew, never leaving his people or the teaching that Messianic Jews should continue to be obedient to the Torah. Clearly, to carry out the call of God, Rabbi *Sha'ul* needed to continue his life as a Torah-observant Jew. As has been noted, "... if he was not scrupulous in his observance of the Torah, he would quickly have been ... disregarded" (in his validity and authority).[1] "... The facts of Paul's continuing conformity to the practices of traditional Judaism are there plainly on the face of Scripture for those willing to find them."[2]

This chapter examines the practices of Rabbi *Sha'ul*. I will concentrate on demonstrating his Torah observance during his journeys outside the land of Israel. Many people take this fact for granted; others think that when Rabbi *Sha'ul* began to believe in Yeshua he abandoned keeping the Torah, especially during his foreign journeys. Still others give Rabbi *Sha'ul* a type of schizophrenic existence, where sometimes he kept the Torah (when with Jews), and sometimes he didn't (when with non-Jews).

Sha'ul and *Hananyah*

When we first meet *Rav Sha'ul* as a Messianic Jew, he is prayed for by another Messianic Jew named *Hananyah* (Ananias; see Acts 9:10–19).

Hananyah was a strict, Torah-observant Messianic Jew, as we see in Acts 22:12–13: "A man named Hananyah, an observant follower of the *Torah* who was highly regarded by the entire Jewish community there [of Damascus], came to me, stood by me and said, 'Brother Sha'ul, see again!' "

By using a known, strictly Torah-observant Messianic Jew to pray for *Sha'ul*, respect, acceptance, halakhic validity, and an immediate rapport were established between the two of them. *Hananyah's* background made him all the more acceptable to Rabbi *Sha'ul* as a bearer of God's message.

Hananyah's example also demonstrates that it was possible to live a Torah-observant Messianic Jewish life. We should expect, then, that Rabbi *Sha'ul*, with a similar background to *Hananyah*, would continue, as *Hananyah* did, to strictly observe the Torah according to his own Pharisaic background. We can make another logical observation here: *Hananyah* continued to observe the Torah when he became a Messianic Jew. If *Hananyah* did this, then *Sha'ul*, who came to faith in Yeshua *after* *Hananyah*, would have also continued to observe the Torah. Therefore, *Hananyah's* lifestyle served as a model for Rabbi *Sha'ul*.

Sha'ul the Messianic Pharisee

Did *Sha'ul* continue his Torah observance after he became a believer in Yeshua? This is a critical question to consider. Rabbi *Sha'ul* made a number of statements that prove his Torah-observant lifestyle.

One of the most important passages to study on the subject is Acts 23:6, where *Sha'ul* says of himself, εγω φαρισαιος ειμι (Greek, *ego Pharisaios eimi*, "I am a Pharisee"). A growing number of people believe that *Sha'ul* never ceased being a Pharisee with regard to his Torah observance. We do not know whether the Pharisee party ever formally expelled *Sha'ul* for his Messianic beliefs. However, according to this passage, *Sha'ul* continued to call himself a Pharisee well after his believing in Yeshua. Let us observe some support for this claim.

First, *Sha'ul* speaks in the present tense. If he had wanted to say that he was no longer a Pharisee, he could have easily done so, but the Greek grammar used here clearly indicates the present tense. In Acts 23, the Pharisees, as a group, stood up for *Sha'ul* when they saw that he shared their doctrinal beliefs and had Pharisaic training. Certainly, this would not have been the case had he no longer been Torah-observant.

Moreover, let me surmise, following the lead of Dr. John Fischer,[3] that *Sha'ul* continued to dress in the recognized Pharisee's "uniform." This would explain why he was easily recognizable as a rabbi and Torah teacher, and thus was invited to speak at a synagogue gathering in Pisidia (see Acts 13:13–43). This is not specifically mentioned in the text, but it does make perfect sense and would be consistent with the picture that we have of Rabbi *Sha'ul.*

In addition, a statement *Sha'ul* made in Acts 28:17 reveals his Torah observance. Either this statement is true, or *Sha'ul* is lying.

> *Sha'ul* called a meeting of the local [Roman] Jewish leaders. . . . He said to them, "I have done nothing against either our people or the traditions of our fathers."

The Greek text renders "the traditions of our fathers" as τοις εθεσι τοις πατρωοις (*tois hethesi tois patroois*). Clearly implied in this wording, are the *mitzvot* of the Torah, and even possibly, the methods of fulfilling the *mitzvot* as developed by the Pharisees. In that era, it would have been considered as acting against the Jewish people if someone practiced and taught an anti-Torah lifestyle. *Sha'ul* states that he did not have that type of an attitude. Furthermore, the record in Acts 21:21–24 clearly confirms that *Sha'ul* kept the Torah, and that the Messianic leaders in Jerusalem expected him to do so. The Messianic leaders instructed *Sha'ul* as follows:

> We have four men [from the Messianic Jewish community in Jerusalem] who are under a vow. Take them with you, be purified with them, and pay the expenses connected with having their heads shaved. *Then everyone will know that there is nothing to these rumors which they have heard about you* [that he teaches against Messianic Jews keeping the Torah]; but that, on the contrary [everyone will know that] you yourself stay in line *and keep the Torah.* (vv. 23b–24, emphasis added)

The text reveals that *Sha'ul* was Torah-observant, and that Messianic Jewish leaders in Jerusalem (who included James, their head rabbi) expected this of him. This leadership insured that *Sha'ul* proved his Torah observance by participating in the ending rituals of a Nazirite vow. This would kill the lie circulating in Jerusalem that he was "teaching all the Jews living among the *Goyim* [Nations] to apostatize from Moshe, telling them not to have a *b'rit-milah* [circumcision] for their sons and not to follow the traditions" (Acts 21:21).

This is significant. The Messianic Jewish leadership in Jerusalem had *Sha'ul* participate in a Nazirite vow sacrifice at the Temple in order to prove that he was Torah-observant. The book of Acts tells us that the rumor that *Sha'ul* taught against the Torah was a lie. Certainly, if *Sha'ul* believed that observing the Torah was wrong, he would not have followed the recommendation of James and the other Messianic Jewish leaders of Jerusalem. He would not have participated in rituals which took place at the end of Nazirite vows.[4] This is strong proof of his attitude toward the Torah. In addition, it demonstrates that he shared the position of the Messianic Jewish leadership, including James, regarding the validity of the Nazirite vow, which is a Torah-mandated *mitzvah* (see Num. 6:1–23).

Sha'ul the Emissary

Let us now look at the foreign journeys of Rabbi *Sha'ul*. First, it is relevant to say that, as a Pharisee, *Sha'ul* would have been familiar with the concept of traveling far and wide to share a religious message. The first-century Pharisees were active in sending emissaries abroad (outside of Judea, Samaria, and Galilee) to share their teachings with Diaspora Jewish communities. In addition, they also traveled around the Land of Israel, teaching and recruiting students for their *yeshiva*s in Jerusalem. For that reason, perhaps, it was not strange for *Sha'ul* to be asked to teach, in Acts 13, at Antioch in Pisidia, where he arrived at the synagogue and was identified as a Pharisee, and perhaps, immediately thought of as a Pharisaic emissary.

At the beginning of his first journey as a Messianic Jewish emissary, Rabbi *Sha'ul* and his companion, Barnabas, traveled to Cyprus. First, they sought out the local Jewish community in order to share their message: "They began proclaiming the word of God in the synagogues" (Acts 13:5).

Not only in Cyprus, but also later on during the same journey in southern Turkey, *Sha'ul* first sought to share the Gospel message with his own people. This is, again, consistent with the Pharisaic practice of teaching in Diaspora Jewish communities. He kept the Sabbath according to local custom, as we see in Acts 13:14b–15: "On the Sabbath they went into the synagogue and sat down. After the reading of the Law and the Prophets, the synagogue officials sent to them, saying . . ."

Fischer points out that *Sha'ul*'s very attire attested to his keeping of Jewish custom: "In Acts 13:15, he [*Sha'ul*] is invited to speak in the synagogue because he is recognized as a religious leader . . . by his [Pharisaic party] dress, a matter of tradition."[5]

Sha'ul then continued with his דרשה (Hebrew, *d'rashah*, sermon).[6] The point is that Rabbi *Sha'ul* (and also Barnabas) kept the Sabbath while sharing the message of Yeshua as the Messiah. In keeping with the local Jewish custom, the Jewish community gathered on the next Sabbath. *Sha'ul* and Barnabas were among them, observing the Sabbath with them (see Acts 13:44–47). Due to the nature of his Torah-based message, as well as being a visiting Pharisee from Israel, *Sha'ul* was again given the honor of speaking freely to the people on this particular *Shabbat*. This highlights the pattern of Rabbi *Sha'ul* and Barnabas in the book of Acts—they kept the Sabbath. They freely shared the Gospel with non-Jews (see Acts 13:48; 14:1, 11 ff.). This was in keeping with what had happened previously (see Acts 10).

The evidence confirms that *Sha'ul* and Barnabas continued to live as Torah-observant Messianic Jews. They were sent to Cyprus to share the news of the Messiah with their Jewish kinsmen, as well as with non-Jews. Again, the Pharisees were very much an emissary type of organization, believing in winning proselytes to Judaism. This was not a new concept to *Sha'ul*. He was sent out as an emissary in Acts 13 by Messianic Jews, as a Messianic Jew, sharing the message of Israel's Messiah. Therefore, it follows that we would expect him to live as a Jew.

If Rabbi *Sha'ul* had any problem with the validity of Torah observance, we would expect to see him shunning the observance of the Sabbath on his journeys. Instead, the record reveals a constant keeping of the Torah, both at Antioch and at Iconium. To have kept parts of the Torah and to have shunned others would be tantamount to an inconsistent, dishonest approach by *Sha'ul*. Therefore, we may conclude that he and Barnabas kept not only the Sabbath, but the other *mitzvot* of the Torah as well.

On Rabbi *Sha'ul*'s second journey as an emissary, this pattern of Torah observance continued. We first see this in the circumcision of *Sha'ul*'s student, Timothy. Acts 16:3 gives us *Sha'ul*'s rationale for the circumcision. It states that *Sha'ul* wanted Timothy to accompany him on his journey as an emissary. He took him and performed a circumcision because of the Jews living in those areas, for they all knew that Timothy's father had been a Greek.

The given rationale has nothing to do with Timothy's entrance into the kingdom of God. Timothy was already identified as a follower of Yeshua in Acts 16:1. However, the local Jewish custom and interpretation of the Torah identified Timothy as a Jew, since his mother was Jewish. Therefore, Timothy needed to be brought into the Abrahamic and Mosaic Covenants in order to live his life as a Messianic Jew, not giving any offense to the local Jewish communities. Professor L. H. Schiffman noted that, according to both the *Mishnah* (*Kiddushin* 3:12–4:14) and first-century rabbinic consensus, if a Jewish male fathered a child with a non-Jewish mother, the child was not Jewish. Conversely, if a Jewish mother gave birth to a child by a Gentile father, the offspring fit into the legal category of a ממזר (Hebrew, *mamzer*, an illegitimate child) according to *Tosefta Kiddushin* 4:16.

If a non-Jew or slave had intercourse with a Jewish woman, and she gave birth to a child, the offspring is a "*mamzer*" [the legal category quoted above].

Professor Schiffman dated this *mishnah* from approximately 125 C.E., and held that its *halakhah* was valid during the first century. A *mamzer* was thus a Jew, though one not given full legal rights. Schiffman noted, "We must remember that *mamzerim* [plural] are considered full fledged Jews from all points of view except that of marriage law."[7]

Another proof of Jewish identity being determined in this era by the mother's identity is given to us in the *Mishnah*:

King Agrippas stood and received the decision of the sages. And when it arrived, it was not able to be given to him, as a foreigner. His eyes welled up with tears. But they said to him, "Do not fear, Agrippas, you are our brother, you are our brother, you are our brother." (*Sotah* 7:8)

This *mishnah* speaks of King Agrippa II (d. 92 C.E.), who was half Jewish through his mother, Cypros. He is clearly pronounced Jewish in this *mishnah* by the sages, who would not have done so if the *halakhah* was not decided in this direction. Schiffman even theorized that this *halakhah* had been accepted for 400 years by the first century C.E. He summarized his finding as follows: "By the time of the rise of Christianity, the *halakhah* had clearly defined the Jew by birth as one who was born to a Jewish mother."[8]

With Timothy falling into this category, Powlison noted, "Jewish custom identified Timothy as Jewish, and his circumcision as a violation to be rectified. From the point of view of the Gospel alone, there was no need to bring Timothy into the Covenant."[9] Since Timothy was a Jew according to first-century interpretation of the Torah, he was summarily circumcised and obliged to fully live as a Jew (see Gal. 5:3). As Powlison further noted:

Paul circumcised Timothy for the sake of the Jews . . . (of) Derbe and Lystra. They were . . . aware of the fact that Timothy's Greek father had not allowed him to be circumcised. In doing so, Paul was showing his respect for Jewish rabbinical opinion, which . . . held that since Timothy's mother was Jewish, Timothy was also: and that it was Paul's responsibility, as Timothy's Jewish authority, to circumcise him. If rabbinic opinion had no authority for Paul, he would have refused to allow Timothy to be circumcised, as he did with Titus.[10]

If Rabbi *Sha'ul* did not respect the Torah, then he would have had no reason to circumcise Timothy. The Torah is clear that every Jewish male needs to be circumcised (see Gen. 17:10–14). *Sha'ul*, in circumcising Timothy, was respecting and keeping the Torah. He was also being sensitive to the consensus of the local Jewish community, which formed its opinion on this issue according to its interpretation of the Torah.

Sha'ul was upholding the principles he brought forth in his teachings. In 1 Corinthians 7:17–18, *Sha'ul* called upon believers to continue being a part of their people after coming to faith in Yeshua as the Messiah. For Timothy to do this, circumcision was required. If *Sha'ul* believed that it was wrong for Messianic Jews to observe the Torah, he would not have circumcised Timothy. In this act of circumcision alone, we see *Sha'ul*'s continued observance of the Torah.

Torah Observance in Philippi

In Acts 16, we find *Sha'ul* in the city of Philippi, in the northeast corner of Macedonia. We read in 16:13 that while at Philippi, *Sha'ul* and his entourage again observed the Sabbath: "Then on *Shabbat*, we went outside the gate to the riverside, where we understood a *minyan* [Jewish prayer group] met."

Simply put, while sharing the message of Yeshua's Messiahship in Philippi, *Sha'ul* kept the Sabbath according to local custom, meeting outside the city. His Sabbath observance continued on this journey as an emissary. The passage describes Rabbi *Sha'ul*'s sojourn in Philippi with a woman named Lydia (see vv.14–15). Questions have been raised as to whether *Sha'ul* and his entourage could have kept ritually clean while staying at Lydia's house. Many people will say that *Sha'ul* had to compromise his Jewish lifestyle and would have been forced to stop eating only kosher food (as found in Lev. 11). However, as I will discuss later, Lydia was called a σεβομενη τον θεον (Greek, *sebomene ton Theon*) in Acts 16:14b. The meaning of this Greek phrase, Godfearer (Hebrew, גרי השער, *gerey hasha'ar*), is crucial to our understanding of both Lydia's identity and of *Sha'ul*'s Torah observance. In her essay on first-century categories of Gentiles and converts, Patrice Fischer identified this term as referring to "that special group of Gentiles who worshiped in synagogues and adopted a Jewish belief system and a Jewish lifestyle for themselves, stopping just short of formal conversion."[11]

This term, then, refers to Gentiles who had faith in the God of Israel, and who maintained a ritually clean and kosher environment in their homes. Fischer also noted that they were a very important part of Diaspora Jewish communities (that is, Jewish communities existing outside of the Land of Israel). This is evident from Lydia's important role in her Jewish community. Powlison also noted that there is no recorded protest from the Jewish community of Philippi, or the surrounding area, over their (*Sha'ul* and his entourage's) behavior.[12] Had *Sha'ul* and his entourage stayed in a ritually defiling environment, we would expect that some kind of protest over their disregard for the Torah and Jewish customs would have been lodged by the local Jewish community. At the least, this would have been a major hindrance to their ability to communicate their message to their kinsman.

Additionally, why would Lydia have been one of those gathered at the riverside on the Sabbath if she were not Torah-observant? The narrative would not make sense if she were not Torah-observant as a "Godfearer." Therefore, we see that Rabbi *Sha'ul* upheld his Torah-observant lifestyle while at Philippi under the care and sponsorship of Lydia. After his release from prison, *Sha'ul* returned to his ritually Jewish environment at Lydia's house. Finally, had *Sha'ul* stayed in a non-kosher environment at Philippi, he could not, in good conscience, have stated what he did in Acts 28:17. The implications of that verse will be discussed in a subsequent section of this work.

Torah Observance in Prison

Acts 16:21–36 presents a problematic but not unsolvable situation regarding *Sha'ul*'s Torah observance. After his miraculous release from prison (see Acts 16:26–28) and the coming to faith of the jailer (see vv. 28–34), *Sha'ul* was taken to the jailer's house and attended to (see vv. 33–35). On the surface, it appears that *Sha'ul* willingly stayed in a non-kosher environment, and ate there as well. It seems as if he broke the *mitzvot* of the Torah. However, *Sha'ul* was following allowances from Jewish custom and first-century rabbinic interpretation of the Torah in his situation.

Although *Sha'ul* was freed from his chains by a supernatural intervention, he continued to submit himself to the jailer as to his governmental authority. He did not flee from the jailer and escape. He also did not encourage the jailer's suicide attempt (see vv. 27–28). Verses 35 and 36 show that *Sha'ul* considered himself to be a prisoner of the Roman authorities until he was officially released (the next day at dawn; see v. 35). *Sha'ul* could have escaped, especially if the jailer had taken his own life, but *Sha'ul*'s respect for authority and for life itself, would not allow him to do so.

Concerning his motivation for his action, *Sha'ul* did not deviate from acceptable Jewish practice by going to the jailer's non-Jewish house. According to this era's rabbinic *halakhah*, because *Sha'ul* was a prisoner of Gentiles, he was allowed to eat non-kosher food as a concession, in order to preserve his life. Remember that he had been severely beaten (see v. 23), so eating was all the more necessary to prevent worsening of his physical condition. As Powlison observed, "While in custody, Jews were allowed, if necessary, to eat forbidden food; if it were possible, however, they arranged to have food brought to them by Jewish friends" (see Acts 14–16; 23:16; 24:23; 27:3; 28:10).[13]

Sha'ul would not have freely chosen to be in ritually unclean surroundings. Given the circumstances, this non-kosher environment did not cancel out *Sha'ul*'s commitment to his Torah observance. We continue to see a consistent, Torah-abiding lifestyle. In this case, a halakhically permissible option was taken, given the circumstances. If this were not so, in Acts 28:17, *Sha'ul* could not have stated, "I have done nothing against either our people or the traditions of our fathers" (Greek, εγω ουδεν εναντιον ποιησας τω λαω ηε τοις εθεσι τοις πατρωοις, *ego ouden henantion poiesas to lao he tois hethesi tois patroois*).

In Acts 17, *Sha'ul* demonstrated his consistent Torah-observant behavior while in Thessalonica, "According to his usual practice, Sha'ul went in; and on three *Shabbatot* [Sabbaths] he gave them *drashot* from the *Tanakh*" (v. 2). In this text, *Sha'ul*'s consistent pattern was to observe the Sabbath according to local custom. Likewise, upon arriving in Berea, it is recorded, "As soon as they arrived, they went to the synagogue" (Acts 17:10). As a side benefit of going to the synagogue, they were often invited to Jewish homes, which provided a ritually fit environment (as with Jason in Acts 17:7 and the previously mentioned Lydia in Acts 13).

At *Sha'ul*'s next destination, Athens, he continued his typical pattern by fellowshipping and teaching in the synagogue (see 17:17). In Corinth, his destination after Athens, this pattern continued. He "stayed on" with the Messianic couple Priscilla and Aquila (see 18:3). The Greek word used for "stayed on" is εμενεν (*hemenen*), giving the sense of "dwelling with" or "living with." By having the same trade (see 18:3b) and Messianic Jewish faith, *Sha'ul* was able to have a ritually kosher environment by living and working with Priscilla and Aquila. In Corinth, also, *Sha'ul* kept his Torah-observant lifestyle. We read in 18:4, "[*Sha'ul* held] discussions every *Shabbat* in the synagogue." Verse 7 of this same chapter reveals *Sha'ul*'s concern for living in a ritually kosher environment: "So he left them and went into the home of a 'God-fearer' named Titus Justus, whose house was right next door to the synagogue."

The Greek word for "next door" in verse 7, is συνομορουσα (*sunomorousa*). It means to "border on (something)."[14] In the Mediterranean world of that day (as today), it was common for a synagogue to adjoin another building. I suspect that is the case here. If *sunomorousa* has its cognate in the Hebrew word, סָמוּךְ (*samukh*), then Justus was a Godfearer who lived right next to the synagogue. Additionally, Justus would have lived as a Jew and kept the *mitzvot*.[15] Note the Greek term applied to Justus: *sebomenou ton Theon* (see 18:7). This is the same category to which Lydia and Cornelius belonged—Gentiles who lived as Jews in ritually fit environments.

Here, some have seen that *Sha'ul* departed from Priscilla and Aquila's company and lodging and moved in with Gentiles in order to begin his new ministry to the Gentiles (following verse 6). This idea is not consistent with the Scriptures and with what we have already seen of *Sha'ul's* Torah observance. To say that *Sha'ul* abandoned his people and customs is an inaccurate interpretation of this verse. Justus provided a ritually fit environment for *Sha'ul* during his year and a half stay in that city. As Powlison noted, "Justus' house was next to the synagogue." Second, *Sha'ul* and his party stayed there for a year and a half with no recorded objections to their conduct [from the Corinthian Jewish community]."[16]

We also see *Sha'ul* ending his second journey as an emissary in Ephesus with further proof of his Torah observance. "He himself [*Sha'ul*] went into the synagogue and held dialogue with the Jews. When they asked him to stay with them longer, he declined" (Acts 18:19–21).

The Jewish community at Ephesus would not have been impressed with a Torah-breaking Jew. If *Sha'ul* had not observed the Torah, he would not have been invited back to speak and teach as a rabbi. This community's openness to *Sha'ul* was related to his being Torah-observant. As a learned Pharisee from Israel with a message from the Torah, he would have been received with enthusiasm (at least initially).

The Writings of Rabbi *Sha'ul*

In his writings, *Sha'ul* also upheld the validity and dignity of the Torah. Dutch scholar Peter Tomson, who has thoroughly researched the New Testament writings of *Sha'ul*, sees a number of interesting facts regarding *Sha'ul's* letters. He noted that the book of Romans is structured in a rabbinic manner: "The basic structure of this mediating, interpretative way of thinking [in the book of Romans] is reminiscent of . . . Rabbinic midrash."[17] Furthermore, "Justification theology and *halakhah* exist independently in Paul, and do not exclude one another."[18] In other words, *Sha'ul* wrote about matters that a first-century rabbi would write about; he wrote in the same style that a first-century rabbi would employ.

Tomson observed that the book of 1 Corinthians reflects *Sha'ul's* respect for the Torah. He states, "In 1 Corinthians . . . the Law [Torah] is affirmed as an authoritative source of practical teaching."[19] Tomson cited a number of places where *Sha'ul* referred to the Torah to make his points in the letter to the Corinthians. He noted that *Sha'ul* quoted eight times from the Torah. Twice, *Sha'ul* cited verses from the Torah to support points, and twice he paraphrased sections of the Torah to illustrate his points. In 1 Corinthians, *Sha'ul* referred to the Torah on at least twelve occasions. What kind of attitude would *Sha'ul* have had in order to make so much use of the Torah in this letter? Additionally, Tomson observed similarities between *Sha'ul*'s writings and those of Rabbi Hillel, the famous first-century Pharisaic sage. Tomson stated, "Of special significance for crucial elements of Paul's teaching are similarities with the Hillelite tradition."[20]

This should further cement our understanding of *Sha'ul*'s closeness to the Torah. The first five books of Moses were the foundation of the belief system of Rabbi Hillel's school of thought. That two Pharisaic rabbis, Hillel and *Sha'ul*, had a strong connection to the Torah should not be surprising. The fact of Yeshua's Messiahship did not interfere with *Sha'ul*'s relation to the Torah. This would be an impossibility, as *Sha'ul* looked at Yeshua as being promised in the Torah, and fulfilling the Torah (I stress the word *fulfilling*, and not *canceling*). Professor Santala saw *Sha'ul*'s love for the Torah, and his reliance upon it as his authoritative source, when he wrote:

> He based his entire thinking on the Old Testament writings, and again, he [Paul] accepted only Old Testament teachings as the sole authority [of his values].[21]

The historic dignity of Rabbi *Sha'ul* can only be upheld if he is seen as a Torah-observant rabbi. Any other view casts doubts on the statements he made about himself, and on the truth of Luke's writings. It is such Messianic Jews, believing Gentiles, and other Jewish writers (e.g., Rabbi Pinchas Lapide) who believe in the truth of *Sha'ul*'s statements. Attempts at portraying *Sha'ul* as abandoning the Torah make *Sha'ul* a hypocrite and a liar at worst, and an inconsistent person at best. Let us understand the Torah-observant Messianic rabbi in such a way as to establish the truth of his writings, personal testimony, and lifestyle. Along with Parkes, it is accurate to conclude, "We shall not have understood the meaning of . . . [*Sha'ul*'s writings] until we have found an interpretation consistent with Paul's own belief that he was throughout a loyal and observant Jew."[22]

Sha'ul remained a Torah-observant rabbi after he came to believe in Yeshua as the Messiah. Understanding this truth can help us interpret the writings of *Sha'ul*. They do not contradict how he lived. This fact should help us see *Sha'ul* with new eyes, for he loved the Torah and did *not* allow for its cancellation. In fact, as Yeshua, he fought for its correct understanding and use.

CHAPTER SIX

SIMON PETER, YESHUA'S SPECIAL STUDENT

Among Yeshua's students, no one captures my attention more than *Shim'on Kefa* (Simon Peter). This loyal, yet fearful, student of Yeshua has similarly impressed many who study the New Testament writings. He is often seen as an outspoken, impetuous person and somewhat of a "klutz."[1]

I see *Shim'on* as Yeshua's Torah-observant תלמיד חכם, (*talmid hakham*). *Talmid hakham* is a Hebrew technical term meaning the leading student (of a rabbi). Every famous rabbi who daily taught the same students had a *talmid hakham*, his chief student. This is the student who figured most prominently in narratives about his rabbi. In first-century Judaism, the chief student was trusted by his rabbi to learn and pass on the rabbi's teachings. The Talmud provides an example of this type of relationship:

> Rabbi Yohanan ben Zakkai had five [primary] students: They were: Rabbi Eliezer ben Hyrkanos, Rabbi Yehoshua ben Hananyah, Rabbi Yosi Hakohen, Rabbi Shim'on ben Netanel and Rabbi Elazar ben Arak ... He [Yohanan ben Zakkai] used to say: If all the sages of Israel were on one pan of a balance scale, and Eliezer ben Hyrkanos were on the other, he would outweigh them all. ... If all the sages of Israel, with even Rabbi Eliezer ben Hyrkanos among them, were on one part of the balance scale, and Rabbi Elazar ben Arak were on the other, he would outweigh them all. (*Avot* 2:10)

Rabbi Elazar ben Arak was the *talmid hakham*, the foremost student of the late first-century sage Rabbi Yochanan ben Zakkai. In another section of this Talmud tractate, Rabbi Yohanan ben Zakkai posed questions to his students, much as Yeshua did to his disciples:

> Go out and discern which is the proper path for a man to cling to. . . . Rabbi Elazar [ben Arak] answered: A good heart. Rabbi Yohanan ben Zakkai said . . . I prefer the words of Elazar ben Arak [to the answers of the other students]. (*Avot* 2:13)

Rabbi Elazar is praised by his teacher, Rabbi Yohanan ben Zakkai, for his wise answers. Elazar was the *talmid hakham*, the one looked up to by the other students, and in some sense the favorite student of his rabbi. In a similar way, *Shim'on* filled this customary role in the rabbinic world by serving in a like capacity to his rabbi, Yeshua. We see that *Shim'on* was considered within the inner circle of Yeshua's best students in Luke 8:51, where Yeshua allowed only Shim'on and two other esteemed students—John and James—to witness a miracle.

In addition, Luke 9:28 gives us one example where Yeshua took only *Shim'on*, John, and James to a secluded place to pray with him. In Luke 22:8, Yeshua sent *Shim'on* and John to carry out a special task. It is *Shim'on* who is given the rabbi's questions in John 21:15–20. It is also *Shim'on* who is singled out by Yeshua as prominent among the students with these words, " 'I also tell you this: you are Kefa [which means 'Rock'], and on this rock I will build my Community, and the gates of Sh'ol [Hell] will not overcome it' " (Matt 16:18).

However we interpret this verse, it is clear that *Shim'on* held a role, if not *the* role, of prominence among Yeshua's students.[2] I am not inferring that *Shim'on* was a better human being by being a *talmid hakham*. None of the famous rabbis' students who functioned in this role were ever considered better human beings than their fellow students. In John 18:10, *Shim'on* took upon himself, the role of defender (or bodyguard) of his rabbi, and thereby lopped off the ear of the High Priest's servant. *Shim'on* considered himself the student who would stick by his rabbi at all costs, and even defend him through force.

Any rabbi's *talmid hakham* would have viewed his rabbi as a role model and would have closely followed his teachings. This is the way the world of rabbis and their students functioned in first-century Israel. If Yeshua taught that the Law and the Prophets were still valid (see Matt. 5:17–19), his students (especially the *talmid hakham*) would learned and taught the same.

Shim'on's Torah Observance

I will comment on a few examples from the life of *Shim'on* regarding keeping the Torah commandments. One prominent situation is in Luke 22:7 ff. Here, Yeshua kept the pilgrimage feast of Passover. *Shim'on* was with Yeshua, and so he kept the feast as well. The keeping of this feast is a *mitzvah* of the Torah (see Lev. 23:4–8; Num. 9:1–14; Deut. 16:1–8). Let us also note that the Torah commandment of Exodus 23:17 was kept here (all males must make the pilgrimage to Jerusalem to celebrate Passover). By associating with Yeshua, *Shim'on* kept a Torah-observant lifestyle.

In Acts 2:1, we find *Shim'on* keeping a Torah commandment by being in Jerusalem for the pilgrimage feast of *Shavu'ot* (see Lev. 23:15–22). It may be argued that Shim'on was keeping *Shavu'ot* almost by coincidence, since he was in Jerusalem anyway, according to Yeshua's instructions (see Acts 1:4). Nevertheless, he fulfilled a Torah commandment by his presence in Jerusalem. It is also not coincidental that Yeshua filled the Messianic Jews with the Holy Spirit in Jerusalem during the *Shavu'ot* festival.[3] In Acts 3, *Shim'on* showed his familiarity with the Torah when he used a verse from Deuteronomy in his public speech about the role of Yeshua as Messiah: "For Moshe himself said, '*Adonai* [God] will raise up for you a prophet like me from among your brothers. You are to listen to everything he tells you' " (v. 22).

If *Shim'on* had a problem with the validity of the Torah after becoming a Messianic Jew, he certainly would not have quoted from it to prove his points. Additionally, *Shim'on* showed his acceptance of the Torah when he stated, "You [Israel] are included in the covenant which God made with our fathers when he said to Avraham, 'By your seed will all the families of the earth be blessed' " (v. 25).

Shim'on referred to the fact that the promises of God to Abraham were inherited by the Jewish people of his day. Where does one learn of this covenant, and of the subsequent Mosaic covenant that God made with the Jewish nation? *In the books of the Torah!* Clearly, *Shim'on* would not have quoted from a body of Scripture that he did not accept as valid.

Shim'on's writings also give us an opportunity to see his attitude toward the Torah. In 1 Peter 1:15, *Shim'on* quoted from the book of Leviticus, "Be holy because I am holy" (11:44; 19:2; 20:7).

Again, by quoting from the Torah, *Shim'on* showed that he accepted the Torah as God's revelation to Israel and all of mankind. Since Yeshua taught (see John 10:35) that all Scripture is to be received as a body and "cannot be broken" (Greek, ου δυναται λυθηναι η γραθη, *ou dunatai luthenai he graphe*), it is certain that *Shim'on* had the same attitude. By teaching this, Yeshua presented the Jewish concept of a book of Scripture that does not contain any division into valid and invalid parts. All Scripture, in Jewish eyes, is valid. In Yeshua's day, the Scriptures included all of the Torah, the Prophets, and the great majority of the Writings (Wisdom Literature). *Sha'ul* taught, "Everything written in the past [in the Scripture] was written to teach us" (Rom. 15:4). The Torah, with all of its commandments, was considered to be valid Scripture by Yeshua, *Sha'ul*, and by *Shim'on*.

In 1 Peter 1:17, *Shim'on* said that God is the Father "who judges impartially according to each person's actions." He also stated this concept in Acts 10:34. Where would *Shim'on* have learned this? *From the Torah*, for Deuteronomy 16:19 directs, "You are not to distort justice or show favoritism" (Hebrew, לא תכיר פנים, *lo takir panim*).

In Hebrew, this particular concept of impartial judgment is called both משוא פנים (*maso panim*) and הכר פנים (*haker panim*). *Shim'on* showed his familiarity with this idea, which is based on the teachings of the Torah. The Jewish Scriptures contain many descriptions of the impartiality of God's judgments, and the need for people to give similar impartial judgments. For example, 2 Chronicles 19:7 declares, "ADONAI our God does not allow dishonesty, partiality or bribe-taking" (Hebrew, משוא פנים, *maso panim*).

We have two more examples in Proverbs: "Showing partiality in judging [Hebrew, הכר פנים, *haker panim*] is not good" (24:23); "To show partiality [Hebrew, הכר פנים, *haker panim*] is not good" (28:21a). *Shim'on* would have understood this concept because of his familiarity with the Torah. This concept was unique to the God of Israel, as other Middle Eastern religious practices of the time did not emphasize the impartial judgment of God or man.[4]

Shim'on further reinforced what the Torah teaches by summing up a lesson from the lives of Abraham and Sarah (see 1 Pet. 3:5). This shows us his respect for the Torah and his use of its narratives as teaching tools.

In 1 Peter 3:8 and 4:8, *Shim'on* expounded on what the Torah teaches in Leviticus 19:18b. He was not making up a new commandment; rather, he was simply rephrasing one of the central commandments of the Torah.

Critics of *Shim'on*'s obedience to the Torah will argue that *Shim'on* was told by God to stop keeping the kosher dietary laws in Acts 10. However, this is simply *not* what the text says. The narrative states:

> Kefa [*Shim'on*] went up onto the roof of the house to pray. He began to feel hungry . . . he fell into a trance in which he saw heaven opened, and something that looked like a large sheet being low-

ered to the ground. . . . In it were all kinds of four-footed animals, crawling creatures and wild birds. Then a voice came to him, "Get up, Kefa, slaughter and eat!" But Kefa said, "No, sir! Absolutely not! I have never eaten food that was unclean. . . ." The voice spoke to him a second time: "Stop treating as unclean what God has made clean." This happened three times, and then the sheet was immediately taken back up into heaven. Kefa was still puzzling over the meaning of the vision he had seen. (vv. 9b–17)

It is interesting to note that *Shim'on* did not, immediately, interpret this dream literally. He did not, according to the text, draw the conclusion that he should stop eating kosher food. Instead, he was puzzled about its meaning. We can be thankful that the book of Acts interprets his vision for us in the continuation of the text. Acts 10:28 describes *Shim'on*'s conclusion of the message of the vision:

He [Kefa] said to them, "You are well aware that for a man who is a Jew to have close association with someone who belongs to another people . . . is something that just isn't done. But God has shown me not to call any *person* common or unclean [non-kosher]. (emphasis added)

The vision, according to *Shim'on*'s own words, had everything to do with showing *Shim'on* that he should share the message of Israel's Messiah with Gentiles. It had nothing to do with breaking the kosher dietary laws of the Torah.[5] *Shim'on* said that he had never broken the kosher dietary laws. This would certainly mean, at a minimum, that he had *never* eaten any food that was prohibited in Leviticus 11. By *Shim'on*'s own words, he had scrupulously kept the Torah with regard to his diet.

In fact, this situation is all the more interesting in that Cornelius, according to the Acts 10 text, was a Godfearer. Again, these were Gentiles who worshipped Israel's God and kept Jewish customs to the extent of having fully kosher (halakhically fit) homes. As I brought out with Lydia and Justus, one had to keep the kosher dietary laws in order to be in this class of Godfearers. Therefore, for *Shim'on* to stay at Cornelius' house and eat there would not have posed any dietary problems for him. Patrice Fischer stated:

The "bottom line" of observance for Gentiles in the Jewish world of Second Temple Judaism would have been the seven Noachide commandments. Godfearing Gentiles, however, went even further, observing the Sabbath, keeping dietary laws (as they were understood then), plus other Jewish observances that they had been taught by their local Jewish leaders.[6]

Shim'on demonstrated his respect for the Torah by using it as a source for his teaching. In 1 Peter 2:9 he used the terms "chosen people, the King's *cohanim* [priests], a holy nation." These terms are first found in the language of Exodus 19:5–6. The following table illustrates how *Shim'on* used the Hebrew words and terms from Exodus 19:5–6 in 1 Peter 2:9.

Comparisons from Shim'on's Letter

Exodus 19:5–6 Hebrew term	1 Peter 2:9 Greek term	English term
סגולה מכל העמים (s'gulah mikol ha'amim)	γενος εκλεκτον (genos eklekton)	a chosen people
ממלכת כהנים (mamlekhet kohanim)	βασιλειον ιερατευμα (basileon hierateuma)	kingdom of priests
גוי קדוש (goy kadosh)	εθνος αγιον (ethnos hagion)	a holy people

The words used in 1 Peter 2:9 are quotes that show an intimate familiarity with the Torah. Additionally, *Shim'on* used quotes in 1 Peter from Isaiah on at least seven occasions, and from the Psalms on at least five occasions. He quoted from the book of Proverbs on another three occasions. The conclusion we must draw is that his source for his letter (1 Peter) is the Torah, as well as the Prophets and the Writings. There is great similarity in terminology and concepts between 1 Peter 2:9 and Exodus 19:5–6. This demonstrates that the letter of 1 Peter, although preserved in Greek, is filled with Torah concepts. *Shim'on*'s second letter (2 Peter) reveals much the same pattern. At three points he quoted from the Scriptures (Psalms, Proverbs, Isaiah). He spoke of the "valuable and superlatively great promises" that God has given Israel (1:4). Where were these promises given? In the Torah!

Shim'on gave the example of Balaam to illustrate the character of false teachers in the early Messianic movement (see 2 Pet. 2:15–16; cf. Num. 22–24). *Shim'on* used another Torah narrative to illustrate a point.

It was by God's word that long ago there were heavens, and there was land which arose out of water and existed between the waters, and that . . . the world of that time was flooded with water and destroyed. (2 Peter 3:5–6)

Shim'on paraphrased from the narratives in the book of Genesis in order to make his points, again showing his respect for the Torah and his belief in the literal truths of the narratives.

My conclusion is that *Shim'on* practiced Torah observance. He learned this from his family, and followed in the Torah-observant footsteps of his rabbi and Messiah, Yeshua. *Shim'on* also showed us great his respect for the Torah in his two letters in the New Covenant—though he did not directly address the question of the role of the Torah in the life of Messianic Jews. This should not surprise us. It is totally consistent with what we should expect, and fits the pattern we have already seen and will continue to see in the lives of the fledgling Messianic Jewish movement of the first century.

CHAPTER SEVEN

TORAH OBSERVANCE IN THE WRITINGS OF JOHN

This next section will focus on the writings of *Yochanan ben Zavdai* (John, son of Zebedee). John's writings are important because he was an eyewitness to Yeshua, a first generation student of the Messiah. Therefore, we can assume that John taught what Yeshua, his rabbi and Messiah, taught him. Note 1 John 1:1, "We have heard him, we have seen him with our eyes, we have contemplated him, we have touched him with our hands!" The eyewitness, firsthand account of John has special significance for us.

> We have Yeshua the Messiah, the *Tzaddik* [Righteous One], who pleads our cause with the Father. Also, he is the *kapparah* [atonement] for our sins—and not only for ours, but also for those of the whole world. (1 John 2:1–2)

Our discussion will focus on the Greek word *dikaion*, used in the text to describe Yeshua as the *Tzaddik*, the Righteous One (Ιησουν Χριστον δικαιον, *Iesoun Christon dikaion*). Does John use word *dikaion* to suggest the cognate Hebrew word *tzaddik*, a technical term for a righteous, strictly Torah-observant man?

First, let us understand that John was raised and steeped in Galilean Jewish culture. He was familiar with the usage and meaning of the word *tzaddik*, as understood in the rabbinic circles of his time. He applied this term to his rabbi, Yeshua. He was calling Yeshua righteous before God. Should a proper rendering of this text be example A or B below?

A. We have an advocate with the Father, Yeshua the Messiah, who is righteous, and he is the propitiation for our sins.

B. We have an advocate with the Father, Yeshua the Messiah, the *Tzaddik*, and he is the propitiation for our sins.

The Greek text of verse 1 states:

παρακλητον εχομεν προς τον πατερα, Ιησουν Χριστον δικαιον, και αυτος ιλασμοςεσ τιν περι των αμαρτιων ημων.

(*parakleton echomen pros ton patera, Iesoun Christon dikaion, kai autos ilasmos estin peri ton hamartion hemon.*)

At first glance, the difference between A and B may seem to be minimal, only a matter of semantics. However, let me argue that in John's culture, such a distinction was important. Although the Greek text has no definite article preceding the word *dikaion*, it is not clear if we are looking at a Greek translation of a Hebrew term and concept. Nevertheless, I will argue from context, usage, and logic, that we are. This is important, in that the Hebrew word *tzaddik* was understood to mean a person who kept a strict Torah-observant lifestyle. In calling Yeshua a *tzaddik*, John was using a technical term that was pregnant with meaning. The Hebrew translation of the New Testament, though a modern one, does justice to this idea when it states:

יש לנו מליס לפני האב ישוע המשיח הצדיק והוא כפרה על חטאינו

Yesh lanu melis lifney ha'av—Yeshua hamashiach, hatzaddik, vehu kapparah 'al hata'eynu. (1 John 2:2)

In English, this is rendered, "We have Yeshua the Messiah, the *Tzaddik*, who pleads our cause with the Father. Also, he is the *kapparah* [atonement] for our sins." By using the definite article in Hebrew before the word *tzaddik*, the translators are conveying an understanding of Yeshua as *The Tzaddik*, which therefore implies that he can cover the world's sins (see 1 John 2:2). Let us now look at what a *tzaddik* is, and note how Yeshua's Torah observance enabled him to fit this description. The *Even-Shoshan Hebrew Biblical Concordance* lists 206 uses of the term *tzaddik*. In most cases, it is used as a noun, though some instances exist where it is used as an adjective. The following chart lists the characteristics of a *tzaddik*, according to the Bible's descriptions. This will help the reader understand the meaning of this word to a first-century Jew. The typical Jewish person of Yeshua's time, especially in Israel (and definitely in Galilee) was familiar with these characteristics, uses, and meanings. In all these instances, the word *tzaddik*, and no other, is used in the original Hebrew text.

The Biblical Verse and the Characteristics of a Tzaddik

Ezekiel 18:5–9	Does not commit idolatry, is not a habitual adulterer, does not break family law *mitzvot* (v. 6).
	Does not economically oppress others, is generous (v. 7).
	Fulfills Exodus 22:25, fulfills *mitzvot* regarding social relations (v. 8).
	Observes *mitzvot* of the Torah (v. 9).
Ezekiel 13:22; Proverbs 13:5	Seeks the truth in all matters.
Ezekiel 3:21	Lives according to the *mitzvot* (does not live lawlessly).
Isaiah 26:7	Principles of living come from God.
1 Kings 8:32	A legally innocent (of breaking the *mitzvot* purposely) Jew.
Habakkuk 2:4	Lives a life of faith in God.
Proverbs 12:5	Thinks of the message of the Torah, and how to apply it in life.
Psalms 32:11; 33:1; 58:10–11; 64:10	Rejoices in God.
Proverbs 18:10; 24:16	Relies on God when in distress.
Proverbs 10:7, 16; 11:30; 23:24; 29:2	His/her life blesses others.

In contrast to a *tzaddik*, the life of an unrighteous man reflects the deeds mentioned in Ezekiel 18:10–13 (murder, theft, defrauding the poor and needy, etc.). Therefore, we can expect that a *tzaddik* was the opposite type of person from the one portrayed in these verses. Instead, a *tzaddik* would live as in verses 15–17. These verses praise the man who משפטי עשה בחוקותי הלך (Hebrew, *mishpatai 'asah b'chukotai halakh*, Ezek. 18:17b). In English this is rendered "executes My ordinances, and walks in My statutes" (18:17b).

In the Bible, the main characteristic of a *tzaddik* is that he is a Torah and *mitzvah*-observant person. The above table is not exhaustive. Yet, we clearly see the characteristics of a *tzaddik*. To summarize, these characteristics were: a Jewish man who kept the *mitzvot*, and who turned to God as his source of life, especially in distress. His life was an example and blessing to others. He was generous with his resources, and sought the truth in all matters. According to this description, it is easy to see how Yeshua fits into this category. He truly was a *tzaddik.*

Joseph *ben Ya'akov,* Yeshua's earthly father, is also identified in Matthew 1:19 as a *tzaddik* (Greek, Ιωσηφ δε ο ανηρ αυτης, δικαιος ων, *Iosef de ho aner autes, dikaios on,* Joseph, her husband, who was righteous). The Hebrew translation of this verse states, יוסף בעלה שהיה צדיק (*Yosef ba'alah shehayah tzaddik,* Joseph her husband, who was a *tzaddik).* Notice, again, the use of the Greek word *dikaios.* Joseph, according to the text, embodied the qualities that made him a *tzaddik.* I am paralleling the Greek word *dikaios* with the Hebrew word *tzaddik.* Louw and Nida defined *dikaios* as "pertaining to being in accordance with what God requires."[1] This is an excellent definition of *tzaddik,* which according to the Scriptures was a Torah-observant person. That a *tzaddik* became a developed and recognized category in rabbinic literature is shown in the Talmud, in tractate *Sanhedrin* 97b. There is a section that discusses the *lamed vavnik.*[2] In a rabbinic discussion on the subject of why the Jews wait upon God for redemption, Rabbi Abaye (d. 339 C.E.) taught, "The world must contain not less than thirty-six righteous men [*tzaddikim*] in each generation who are trusted with the Shekinah's countenance."[3]

Although Rabbi Abaye lived some three centuries after Yeshua, like Yeshua, he lived in an atmosphere steeped in the Torah. We can see that in Abaye's day, discussion about the influence of a *tzaddik* was very much alive.

It is my conclusion that in calling Yeshua a *tzaddik,* John meant that Yeshua was Torah-observant and that he fully embodied the characteristics given in the above chart. Similarly, we find that John's writings reveal his own Torah observance. This is logical, since he portrayed Yeshua as being Torah-observant. John wrote, "Here is how we know that we love God's children: when we love God, we also do what he commands. For loving God means obeying his commands" (1 John 5:2–3).

The Greek word used here to mean "commands" is εντολας (*entolas).* The question we need to answer is whether John uses *entolas* to portray a Greek rendition of the Hebrew concept of *mitzvah.* If so, the meaning is tied to the keeping of the Torah's *mitzvot. Entolas* carries the meaning of *mitzvot* in John's usage here. Six examples from the Septuagint demonstrate this direct *entolas-mitzvot* connection.[4] When Jewish scholars translated the Torah into the Septuagint, they carefully chose the cognate Greek words that expressed the concepts embodied in the Hebrew Scriptures. The following table will demonstrate the comparisons.

Hebrew and Greek Word Usage

Bible Verse	Septuagint Word Used	Torah Word Used
Exodus 24:12	entolas	mitzvah
Deuteronomy 6:25	entolas	hamitzvah
Deuteronomy 8:1	entolas	hamitzvah
Deuteronomy 11:2–8	entolas	mitzvot
Deuteronomy 30:8	entolas	mitzvotav
Deuteronomy 30:10	entolas	mitzvotav

Even if the reader has no knowledge of Hebrew and Greek, the English transliteration reveals much. Each time the term *entolas* is used in the Septuagint, in these six examples, it parallels the Torah's use of the word *mitzvah*. It appears that the Jewish scribes and sages who translated the Septuagint had the concept of the Torah commandments in mind when using the Greek word *entolas*. There is good reason then, for concluding that John used a Hebraic understanding of the word *entolas* in 1 John 5:2–3. He was saying that the proof of showing one's love for God is to keep the *mitzvot* of the Torah.

1 John 5:1 is a passage of Scripture that encourages Messianic Jews to love God in a practical manner. The "how" of loving God is taken up in verses 2–3. He encouraged the Messianic Jewish believers to live out the love God had poured upon them through Yeshua by keeping the *mitzvot* of the Torah. The New Testament authors were not deep mystics with a Hellenistic way of looking at the world. They were Torah-observant Jews, who looked for practical ways to live out the love that was placed in their hearts by their Messiah. Their foundation for living was the Torah. In order to write 1 John 5:1 as an instruction for others, John himself, would have had to have been Torah-observant.

OTHER TORAH-OBSERVANT MESSIANIC JEWS

There are a number of other Messianic Jews in Scripture who were Torah-observant. Although they are not major figures, their lives fit the pattern of Messianic Jewish Torah observance that we have examined. Let us see who these people were, and note their Torah observance.

Hananyah

Hananyah (Ananias) appeared in Acts 9. He was the Messianic believer who delivered the message from God to *Rav Sha'ul*. In recounting the incident, *Sha'ul* stated, "A man named *Hananyah*, an observant follower of the *Torah* who was highly regarded by the entire Jewish community there [in Damascus], came to me" (Acts 22:12).

The Greek text describes *Hananyah* as ευλαβης κατα τον νομον (*eulabes kata ton nomon*). A good Hebrew rendition would be a שומר התורה (*shomer haTorah*).[1] In English, this simply means an "observer of the Torah." *Hananyah*, described by Luke as a Torah-observant Messianic Jew, had no problem with keeping the Torah and believing in Yeshua. His devout Torah observance was probably a reason for the Jewish community's admiration of him (see v. 12). *Hananyah* is a typical example of a Torah-observant Jew in the first Messianic Jewish communities.

The Torah Zealots

Another powerful text describing the presence of Torah-observant Messianic Jews is Acts 21:17–26. In verse 20, the Messianic leaders received *Sha'ul* in Jerusalem, and declared to him, "You see, brother, how many tens of thousands of believers there are among the Judeans, and they are all zealots for the *Torah*."

The Greek text calls these thousands of believers ζηλωται του νομου (*zelotai tou nomou*), which the *Complete Jewish Bible* correctly renders "zealots for the Torah." It is estimated that the population of Jerusalem in the first century C.E. was approximately 100,000 to 120,000 people. In Acts 21:20, the Greek text literally tells us that "tens of thousands" (μυριαδες, *muriades*, myriads) of Torah-observant Messianic Jews lived in Jerusalem. Using the least case scenario, at least 20,000 people in this population were Torah-observant Messianic Jews. There were possibly even more, according to the text. The common perception of first century C.E. Jerusalem is that the population was hardhearted toward Yeshua and the Messianic movement. However, I believe that whenever close to twenty percent of a population believes in Yeshua, a revival is at hand.

Two Messianic Pharisees

Two prominent Pharisees who were Torah-observant and Messianic were Joseph from Arimathea and Nicodemus. Of Nicodemus we read, "There was a man among the *P'rushim* [Pharisees], named Nakdimon [Nicodemus], who was a ruler of the Judeans" (John 3:1). At the very least, we know that Nicodemus was a Pharisee. As such, he would have been a scrupulous keeper of the *mitzvot* of the Torah, probably according to the teaching of either Hillel or Shammai.[2] He would also have been a strict keeper of Jewish customs and the kosher dietary laws, according to the oral tradition of the Pharisees. John 19:39–42 shows that this man was a believer in Yeshua. Moreover, there is no record of him renouncing his Pharisaic ways, nor would we expect him to have done so.

Joseph is mentioned in a number of places in the Gospels. One of them is Luke 23:50, where we learn that he was a member of the Sanhedrin in Jerusalem. Therefore, he had to have been a strictly Torah-observant Jew. Luke used the Hebrew technical term, *tzaddik* (in the Greek text, δικαιος, *dikaios*). As we have seen previously, the use of this term implies that Joseph was a scrupulously Torah-observant Jew. Again, this is consistent with the picture of the first generation of Messianic Jews. Matthew confirmed that Joseph was "himself a *talmid* [disciple, student] of Yeshua" (27:57).

Messianic Women

In Luke 23:56b, we are presented with an interesting fact:

> On *Shabbat* [the Sabbath] the women [who had come with Yeshua from Galilee] rested, in obedience to the commandment.

Also note Mark 16:1–2a:

> "When *Shabbat* was over, Miryam [Mary] of Magdala, Miryam the mother of Ya'akov [James], and Shlomit [Salome] bought spices in order to go and anoint Yeshua. Very early on Sunday, just after sunrise, they went to the tomb."

Although a crisis had just occurred in their lives, these women believers in Yeshua observed the Sabbath. They did not attempt to work on Yeshua's corpse until after the Sabbath had passed. We would expect this, as Yeshua would have lived a life consistent with such Torah observance and they would have followed his example. Had Yeshua not lived a life consistent with such Torah observance, so many Jews would not have recognized him as the Messiah.

The evidence of *Hananyah*, the tens of thousands of Messianic Jerusalemites, Joseph of Arimathea, Nicodemus the Pharisee, and the women disciples of Yeshua confirm the existence of Torah-observant, Messianic Jewish communities.

PART
THREE

REACTIONS TO THE TORAH OBSERVANCE OF YESHUA AND HIS FOLLOWERS

CHAPTER NINE

THE COMMON PEOPLE

As noted previously, at this time, the common people of this region were also Torah-observant. The methods of Torah observance would have varied in each area of Israel, due to both geographic differences and educational emphases. Clearly, if Yeshua had not paid attention to the Torah, he would have found little favor in the eyes of the common people of his country.

How, then, did the common people—the laborers, agricultural workers, fishermen, merchants, tanners, builders and their families—react to Yeshua's life? First, there is no simple answer to this question. There are some notable instances in the New Testament where we can see a reaction. If the common people[1] found fault in Yeshua's Torah observance, we would expect to see some sign of this in the New Testament. Conversely, if Yeshua's Torah observance found favor in the eyes of the common people, we might also hope to see some evidence of this, as well. Therefore, let us take a brief look at the reactions of the common people.

In Luke 4, we see the reaction to Yeshua's teaching by typical Galilean Jews. Luke reported that Yeshua taught in Galilean synagogues in his role as a rabbi. Luke also recorded the people's reactions. Verse 15 notes, "He taught in their synagogues, and everyone respected him."

Additionally, Luke recorded an incident in Nazareth, which was Yeshua's hometown. After he read a passage in the synagogue on a Sabbath, the synagogue attendees had this reaction: "Everyone was speaking well of him and marveling that such appealing words were coming from his mouth" (v. 22).[2]

In verses 31–32, we see the common synagogue attendee's reaction to Yeshua: "He went down to K'far Nachum [Capernaum], a town in the

Galil, and made a practice of teaching them on *Shabbat*. They were amazed at the way he taught, because his word carried the ring of authority."

Later in this chapter, we see again, how the common people felt toward Yeshua: "When day had come, he [Yeshua] left and went away to a lonely spot. The people looked for him, came to him and would have kept him from leaving them" (v. 42).

In the next chapter, Luke presents a similar picture to us. "The news about Yeshua kept spreading all the more, so that huge crowds would gather to listen and be healed of their sicknesses" (5:15). After healing a crippled man, the crowd reacted to Yeshua's actions and teachings. "Amazement seized them all, and they made a *b'rakhah* [blessing] to God; they were awestruck, saying, 'We have seen extraordinary things today'" (v. 26).

In Luke 6, Yeshua received a positive reaction from the crowd of Jews that had gathered from various parts of Israel. It is written, "Great numbers of people from all Y'hudah, Yerushalayim and the coast around Tzur and Tzidon . . . had come to hear him and be healed of their diseases" (v. 17).

The reaction Yeshua received from a Jewish crowd in the Galilean city of Nain after performing a miracle is also recorded in Luke. "They [the citizens of Nain] were all filled with awe and gave glory to God, saying, 'A great prophet has appeared among us,' and, 'God has come to help his people'" (7:16).

These passages in Luke reveal the positive responses of the crowds that followed Yeshua the rabbi. They believed that God was working through Yeshua to encourage them. He was even deemed a great prophet.

In modern Western society, we get a glimpse of how well respected an individual was by attending the funeral and hearing the eulogies of family, friends, and colleagues. It is interesting to note the reaction of the common Jewish pilgrims who were going up to Jerusalem to celebrate Passover at the time of Yeshua's crucifixion. Luke noted the crowd's reaction by writing, "Large numbers of people followed [the Roman death procession to Golgotha], including women crying and wailing over him. . . . And when all the crowds that had gathered to watch the spectacle saw the things that had occurred, they returned home beating their breasts" (23:27, 49).

Beating the chest area with one's fists was a sign both of mourning and that an unjust act had occurred. It is noteworthy that this was the reaction of people who were identified as Jewish "commoners." Some of the derisive reactions toward Yeshua at his death are recorded—mockers taunted him; Roman soldiers ridiculed him; men called αρχοντες

(Greek, *archontes*, unidentified rulers) said negative things about him (see Luke 23:35–38); and a dying criminal insulted him (see v. 39). We should pay attention to the fact that most of these people were not part of the common class of people—certainly, the Roman soldiers, unidentified rulers, and condemned criminals would not be included in this group.

Other positive reactions are noted: another dying criminal reacted positively to Yeshua (see vv. 40–42), and a Roman officer who witnessed the crucifixion had a positive reaction (see v. 47).[3]

The incident recorded in Luke 24:13–32, again, demonstrates a positive reaction to Yeshua by two Judean Jewish men, one named Cleopas. The particular standing these men had in Judean society is not mentioned. However, their reaction to Yeshua's life is typical as recorded by Luke: "Yeshua from Natzeret . . . was a prophet and proved it by the things he did and said before God and all the people" (24:19). If these men were common Jews from the Judean village of Emmaus, their reaction to Yeshua is significant.

These positive reactions would *not* have occurred if Yeshua had been ignorant of the Torah. If he had taught or practiced against the Torah, the common people from both the Galilee and Judea would have dismissed him, his teachings, and his miracles. A Torah-observant rabbi who taught and healed would have been heard and followed. That is precisely the picture we have of Yeshua—a well-respected rabbi, teacher, and healer, as well as a great prophet and the Messiah (see Luke 22:66 ff.).

Matthew recorded similar reactions to Yeshua. "Huge crowds followed him from the Galil, the Ten Towns, Yerushalayim, Y'hudah, and Ever-HaYarden [towns east of the Jordan River]" (4:25). We are twice told that Yeshua had large crowds following him during his teaching in Galilee (see Matt. 8:1, 18). Other verses confirm that Yeshua had a constant crowd around him in Galilee. "When he saw the crowds, he had compassion on them" (9:36). "Many people followed him; and he healed them all" (12:15b). "Such a large crowd gathered around him that he got into a boat and sat there while the crowd stood on the shore" (13:2). "So when he came ashore, he saw a huge crowd; and, filled with compassion for them, he healed those of them who were sick" (14:14). Matthew continued to develop this picture in stating, "Large crowds came to him, bringing with them the [sick] . . . and many others" (15:30).

As stated previously, the people's reaction to this is recorded: "They said a *b'rakhah* [thanksgiving blessing] to the God of Israel" (15:31). Crowds also were common for Yeshua during his time in the area east of the Jordan River. Matthew stated, "[He] traveled down the east side of the Yarden [Jordan] River. . . . Great crowds followed him, and he healed them there" (19:1–2).

Matthew recorded that many Jewish residents in Galilee and in the Jordan Valley were extremely impressed with Yeshua. This reaction could not have occurred unless Yeshua was Torah-observant.

John (Mark), Barnabas' relative, also wrote of Yeshua's life. He describes crowd scenes, much as Matthew does, and is actually more graphic in his portrayal of the intensity of the crowd's fervor to hear and see Yeshua. In Mark 1:37, he recorded that *Shim'on* said to Yeshua (in Galilee), "Everybody is looking for you," in describing the aftermath of a series of healings that Yeshua carried out. He also noted that, "Yeshua could no longer enter a town openly but stayed out in the country, where people continued coming to him from all around" (1:45).

In Mark 3:7, it is recorded that "Yeshua went off with his *talmidim* to the lake [Sea of Galilee], and great numbers followed him from the Galil." Mark 3:19b–20 adds to this picture of Yeshua's immense popularity with the people of Galilee: "Then he entered a house; and once more, such a crowd came together that they couldn't even eat." Mark's description of the setting of the Sermon on the Mount adds to the picture: "The crowd that gathered around him was so large that he got into a boat on the lake and sat there" (4:1).

Other verses in Mark's narrative tell us that crowds accompanied Yeshua wherever he went (see 5:21; 6:34, 44, 54–56; 8:1, 9; 9:14; 10:1, 46; 12:37b). Again, this type of crowd response would only have occurred if Yeshua had been Torah-observant.

We have already discussed how *Yochanan ben Zavdai* portrayed Yeshua. In his narrative of Yeshua's life, he also showed us the common people's positive response to the life and message of Yeshua. He did not, however, emphasize this particular point. We see Yeshua and his students invited to a wedding (see John 2:2). We see a large crowd following him (6:2, 5). These people proclaimed Yeshua as "the prophet" (6:14), a reference to Deuteronomy 18:18–19. "I will raise up for them a prophet like you [Moses] from among their kinsmen. I will put my words in his mouth, and he will tell them everything I order him." This crowd was so impressed by Yeshua that they wanted to make him a king (see John 6:15). John also wrote of the people's desire to pursue Yeshua (although Yeshua questioned their motivation): "They themselves [the crowd] boarded the boats and made for K'far-Nachum in search of Yeshua" (6:24).

John, in particular, related that Yeshua was popular in Galilee. He recorded the fact that the crowd reaction in Judah was more mixed (see 7:10–12). Clearly, there was a positive reaction to his teaching and message in Judah.

Many in the crowd [in Jerusalem] put their trust in him and said, "When the Messiah comes, will he do more miracles than this man has done?" (John 7:31)

On hearing his words, some people in the crowd [in Jerusalem] said, "Surely this man is 'the prophet' "⁴; others said, "This is the Messiah." (7:40)

Additional passages in John's narrative that speak of a positive popular reaction to Yeshua are 8:30, 9:16 (where some of the Pharisees react positively), and 10:41–42. John described mixed reactions to Yeshua by noting, at length, the discussions between Yeshua and some of the religious leaders of Judah (the Sadducees, the High Priest's allies, and those Pharisees who allied themselves with the High Priest's political policies). However, the reaction to Yeshua in Galilee was overwhelmingly positive. In Judah, the reaction to Yeshua ranged from curious to positive among the people, and was mixed among the religious leaders.

To summarize my findings from the four narratives of Yeshua's life, we find that he is portrayed as a popular teacher, rabbi, and healer, particularly in Galilee. Only a Torah-observant rabbi would get such a reaction from the common people.

CHAPTER TEN

JERUSALEM'S RELIGIOUS LEADERS

This chapter will examine the response of the first-century Jerusalem religious authorities to Yeshua and Messianic Judaism. Previously, I commented that a number of scholars view Yeshua as having been in the mold of Pharisaism, particularly that of *Beyt Hillel*. Therefore, it is relevant to examine the reaction of Pharisaic leaders. Additionally, we should look at other religious parties of the time.

For centuries, all of Jerusalem's religious authorities have been stereotyped as enemies of Yeshua. Jacob Neusner notes such stereotyping concerning the Pharisees.

> The New Testament's negative picture [of the Pharisees] was widely produced in Christian preaching, writing, and scholarship. . . . "Pharisee" became a synonym for [a] hypocrite, and "Pharisaism" for formalism.[1]

This chapter will also look at the reaction of Jerusalem's Pharisees, Sadducees, scribes, and priests to the message of Yeshua's Messiahship. It is important to mention that this is a difficult subject to address—for two reasons. First, it is not always easy to precisely identify each group mentioned in the Gospels. A second difficulty is that it is not simple to place each religious leader mentioned in the New Testament into a neatly defined group. However, I will draw general conclusions based on specific evidence.

The Pharisees

In the New Testament, much has been written regarding the Pharisees' reaction to the Gospel message and to Yeshua himself. Who made up this group, the Pharisees? Neusner concluded that the Pharisees were a sect within Judaism whose main criteria were to eat in a state of ritual purity, maintain careful tithing, and observe agricultural offerings. In addition, they held to specific interpretations of how to keep the Sabbath and festival commandments. They showed "cult centered piety . . . [which was reproduced] in the home; [they] attempted to effect the Temple's purity laws at the table of the ordinary Jew."[2]

The Pharisees understood themselves to be the valid interpreters of the Torah, which they saw as the sole basis for governing the Jewish people. They thought of themselves as the inheritors of the authority of Moses, Joshua, the seventy elders, the prophets, and the leaders of the Jewish people in the times of Ezra and Nehemiah. The historian Josephus mentioned that their number prior to 70 C.E. was about 6,000 men.[3] Additionally, they put themselves in the line of those teachers who had been developing the Oral Law well before the first century. Although this sect's founders had been deeply involved in the political life of the Hasmonean Jewish kingdom (about 160 to 66 B.C.E.), by Yeshua's time, they had hoped to restore the people's fortunes through spiritual means.[4] They had been stripped of much of the political power they wielded in the days of Queen Alexandra,[5] who used them as advisors and policymakers. Neusner accurately noted, "It seems likely that to be a Pharisee was not a profession, but an avocation."[6]

In other words, being a Pharisee was not a full-time paid occupation. Rather, the Pharisees were strictly Torah-observant Jews who had certain ritual and philosophical understandings among themselves. Some of the first century's most famous religious teachers came from this sect, such as Hillel, Shammai, and *Gamliel*. These teachers are still honored today for their brilliant interpretations of the Torah, for their service to their people, and for their dedication to teaching the Torah.

The Pharisees looked upon themselves as a continuation of the Torah-teaching profession that was initiated in Israel by the biblical figure Ezra in the fifth century B.C.E. The Talmud tractate, *Pirke Avot*, gives a genealogy of Pharisaic development. It notes that a historical line of Jewish religious leaders upheld and taught the Torah. The following list traces this line.

Historical Line of Teachers According to Tractate Pirke Avot

1. *Moshe* (Moses)
2. Joshua
3. The Elders
4. The Prophets
5. Men of the Great Assembly (the leaders' council initiated by Ezra)
6. Shim'on Ha-Tzaddik

7. Antigonus from Socho
8. The pair of Yossi ben Yoezer and Yossi ben Yohanan
9. The pair of Yehoshua and Nittai
10. The pair of Yehudah ben Tabbai and Shim'on ben Shetach
11. The pair of Shemayah and Avtalyon
12. The pair of Hillel and Shammai

This list demonstrates how the Pharisees viewed their roots. They believed that the Torah, in both written and oral form, was given to Moses on Mt. Sinai. These teachings were passed on to succeeding generations. When Ezra came to Israel, he developed a religious leaders' council (the Great Assembly), which, among other things, was responsible for developing Torah teaching for the returning exiles in Israel. Shim'on Ha-Tzaddik (number 6 on the list) was a member (or a student of a member) of this Assembly. The methods and principles of Torah study were developed and handed down over 500 years. Hillel and Shammai, the last pair listed, were in their prime as the two leaders of the Sanhedrin just a generation before Yeshua. It is even possible that there were a small number of overlapping years in the lives of Hillel, Shammai, and Yeshua.

It is difficult to pinpoint the exact beginning of the Pharisees, as we know them in the New Testament, functioning as an independent religious party. According to Josephus, their actual beginnings were in 160 B.C.E., during the reign of the Hasmonean ruler, Jonathan.

Of importance is the fact that the Pharisees believed their methods of interpreting the Torah were handed down to them through successive generations of Torah teachers, starting with Moses. Although the actual number of Pharisee party members during Yeshua's lifetime was only a few thousand, they were influential as religious leaders and Torah teachers.

The Pharisees had several beliefs that segregated them from other Judean groups, such as the Sadducees. They held the popular belief in the resurrection of the dead and life in the "world to come" and accepted the existence of the unseen spirit world and angelic beings. The Sadducees believed in a physical world that could be seen and not in a "world to come." Additionally, they rejected the authority of the Prophets. The Pharisees accepted the writings of the Prophets as part of the Scriptures.

As previously mentioned, the Pharisees had their own system of ritual purity. Other Jewish groups from this period, such as the Essenes and/or the Qumran community, also had their own systems of ensuring ritual cleanliness. The Pharisees considered ritual purity to be a serious aspect of Torah practice. It was certainly an outstanding feature of their party.

Additionally, the Pharisees were primarily involved in providing Torah education for the layman. Learning and teaching the *mitzvot* (and their interpretation of how to practice the *mitzvot*) was their *raison d'être*. In their view, every Jewish family was able to learn and practice the Torah. They considered it their place to serve their people in Torah education. It was a grass-roots movement in its beginnings. The Sadducees' *raison d'être*, on the other hand, was based on the role of the priesthood in Israel. This party included many priestly families of wealth and status. They believed themselves to be the best interpreters and teachers of Torah, in addition to having the role of the keepers of the Temple, and sole arbitrators of the Temple rituals. Because of the central role of the Temple and its rituals in the life of Israel, the Sadducees felt they were the legitimate authorities regarding the essence of the Torah.

There was, then, a type of rivalry between the two parties, although they both worked together in the Sanhedrin, sometimes more smoothly than at other times.

Pharisaic Reaction in the New Testament

To sum up, the reaction of this sect was mixed. We find much Pharisaic opposition to the person and message of Yeshua. However, we also find individual Pharisees who were true believers in Yeshua, and who were Messianic Jews. If Dr. Fischer's conjecture[7] that Acts 21:20 includes many Messianic Jews who were Pharisee party members is accurate, then our whole picture of their reaction must change. I, along with many other scholars, believe that the Pharisees were divided along political lines on the issue of Messianic Judaism. Those Pharisees from the Hillelite wing of this sect were more favorable toward Yeshua, and those from the Shammaite wing were more negative toward Yeshua. However, the historical picture remains ambiguous. The New Testament does not provide a clear picture of one unified group reaction of the Pharisees toward Yeshua.

Positive Reactions to Yeshua and Messianic Judaism

The New Testament indicates that individual Pharisees were sympathetic to, and followers of, Yeshua. What actually happened to their membership in the sect after their belief in Yeshua is not mentioned. However, it is significant that in Acts 23:6, *Sha'ul* described himself as εγω φαρισαιος ειμι (Greek, *ego pharisaios eimi*). This literally reads, "I *am* a Pharisee" (emphasis added). The Greek language is flexible enough to have offered *Sha'ul* the opportunity to write, "I *was* a Pharisee," if that is what *Sha'ul* intended to say—however, he chose to state this in the present tense. It appears, then, that *Sha'ul* did not sever himself from the Pharisees because of his belief in the Messiah. We will see another instance of this when we focus on *Sha'ul* later in this chapter.

In John 3:1–21, Nicodemus is described as "a man among the *P'rushim* [Pharisees]" (v. 1). He had asked deep and sincere questions of Yeshua. This same Pharisee is presented as one of the two Pharisees who insured a ritually proper burial for Yeshua (see John 19:38–42). This act by Nicodemus was a sign of sympathy toward Yeshua. In addition, John 7:37–52 portrays Nicodemus as arguing in defense of a proper hearing for Yeshua in the midst of considerable opposition. Thus, according to John, Nicodemus was, at least to some extent, a follower of Yeshua. His colleagues' reaction to his actions on behalf of Yeshua is not mentioned in the New Testament. We know of no consequences to Nicodemus' sympathies for Yeshua, such as expulsion from the sect.

Acts 15:5 gives evidence of favorable reaction to Yeshua by some Pharisees. In this text, an unspecified number of Pharisees are included in the Messianic Jewish community at Jerusalem. It states, "Some of those who had come to trust [in Yeshua] were from the party of the *P'rushim.*" Again, we have no further mention of these men, nor any information as to what happened to their membership in the sect.

A most interesting reaction is recorded of *Rabban Gamliel.* In Acts 5:34 ff., the beloved sage advised against trying to snuff out the Messianic movement by force in stating:

> "If this idea or this movement [Messianic Judaism] has a human origin, it will collapse. But if it is from God, you will not be able to stop them; you might even find yourselves fighting God."

The Sanhedrin accepted this sage's opinion. Although *Rabban Gamliel* is not mentioned as a Messianic Jew, he is portrayed as a voice of moderation among the Pharisees. Thus, the stereotype that portrays all Pharisees as opposed to Yeshua is not accurate.

It is also noteworthy that a group of Pharisees warned Yeshua of the danger of his death at the hands of King Herod Antipas (see Luke 13:31 ff.). It is possible that these men were Pharisees from *Beyt Hillel* and, out of a sense of kinship and sympathy to Yeshua, felt it was their duty to warn him. To help us understand how one sect could have such a diverse reaction to Yeshua, let us remember that the Pharisees were not homogeneous in their religious and political belief systems. As Fischer noted, "It must be kept in mind that the Pharisees allowed for considerable diversity among themselves."[8]

In like manner today, it is possible for individual members of the Democratic or Republican parties in the U.S.A. to be on opposite sides of issues such as tax increases, forced busing, quotas in education, and abortion rights—yet, they would all belong to the same political party.

Also significant is the fact that during Yeshua's teaching career, he was welcomed in his role as rabbi-teacher into the house of certain Pharisees. Luke noted three such incidents (see 7:36; 11:37; 14:1). This is revealing, as table fellowship with the Pharisees was a sign of acceptance. The fact that Yeshua was given table fellowship and was even called "rabbi" by the Pharisee Simon confirms that his host considered him legitimately Torah-observant. We can conclude that Yeshua was accepted as Torah-observant and worthy of fellowship by at least some of the Pharisees.

The Pharisees' reaction to the death of James' (Yeshua's brother, *Ya'akov*) is most interesting. The historian Josephus tells us (Antiquities 20:9:1) that the Pharisees defended James' righteous memory and reputation after he was murdered by a conspiracy of Sadducees and Herodian allies. As previously mentioned, James functioned as the chief rabbi of the Jerusalem Messianic community. The fact that there were Pharisees who defended him demonstrates, again, that there was sympathy in their midst for Messianic Judaism. Josephus noted:

> Ananus [the Sadducean High Priest] took before them the brother of Jesus . . . whose name was James . . . he had formed an accusation against [him] as breakers of the Torah, and . . . delivered [James] . . . to be stoned. But as for those who seemed the most equitable of citizens, and such as were the most uneasy at [this] breach of the Torah, they disliked what was done; they also sent to the King [Agrippa], desiring him to send to Ananus that he should act so no more, for that what he had already done was not to be justified . . . Agrippa took the high priesthood from him [Ananus, due to his murder of James].

Finally, we must include *Sha'ul* among the Pharisees who believed in Yeshua, though his circumstances are different than those of all the other Pharisees mentioned. *Sha'ul*, again, did not give up his identification as a Pharisee, even after his belief in Yeshua. In fact, in Acts 23:6–10, *Sha'ul* stated that he considered himself a Pharisee, and the Pharisees who were in the audience showed sympathy for him.

> "I am a Pharisee, a son of Pharisees. . . ." There occurred a dissension between the Pharisees and Sadducees. . . . [T]here occurred a great uproar; and some of the scribes of the Pharisaic party stood up and began to argue heatedly [against the Sadducees], saying, "We find nothing wrong with this man [Paul]." (Acts 23:6, 7, 9)

Again, in Acts 28:17, *Sha'ul* stated, "Brethren, though I had done nothing against our people or the customs of our fathers, yet I was delivered as a prisoner from Jerusalem into the hands of the Romans." If Paul had severed himself from the Pharisees, their customs, and their understanding of the Torah, it is doubtful he could have made the above statement. The point is that *he lived consistently throughout his lifetime.* He remained the Pharisee of Pharisees. While still considering himself a Pharisee, he fervently believed in the Messiah, Yeshua.

Negative Reactions to Yeshua/Messianic Judaism on Behalf of the Pharisees

Pharisaic opposition to both Yeshua and Messianic Judaism appears in the New Testament. Opposition to Yeshua, as found in the New Testament, fits loosely into two categories: that which is based on doctrinal differences, and that which is based on political differences. These differences are demonstrated in the following table.

Table of Opposition

Opposition Built Upon Differences of Torah Interpretation	*Opposition Built Upon Political Alliances and Powers Struggles*
Matthew 9:11 ff. (Luke 5:29–32)	Matthew 16:1 ff.
Matthew 12:1–8 (Mark 2:23 ff.)	Matthew 21:45
Matthew 15:1–14 (Mark 7:1 ff.)	Matthew 22:15
Luke 1:21	Mark 3:6
Luke 7:36–49	Mark 8:11
Luke 11:37–38	Mark 10:2
Luke 15:1–2	Mark 12:13 ff.
Luke 17:20	Luke 11:39–53
Luke 19: 38–40	Luke 16:14
John 9:13–17	John 7:32 ff.
	John 7:45–49
	John 8:3 ff.
	John 9:39
	John 11:46–52
	John 12:19, 42 (implied)
	John 18:3

The New Testament gives ample examples of Pharisaic opposition to Yeshua, with both political and doctrinal motivations as the cause. Some Pharisees had theological and interpretational differences with Yeshua.

Others had political fears and pressures that were their motivation in relating to him.

In the great majority of cases cited above, the individual Pharisee's motivation determined Yeshua's reaction. Nicodemus is pictured as sincerely asking questions. Yeshua answered this Pharisee by sharing the truth of each matter with him. Often, Yeshua left the questioning Pharisee(s) with a strong suggestion to learn how to correctly interpret the Torah, while not directly answering their inquiry. Other Pharisees, who wanted to test, tempt, or embarrass Yeshua, were left without answers to their inquiry, and with rebukes for their improper motivation.

> Then the Pharisees went and plotted together how they might trap Him [Yeshua] in what He said. And they sent their disciples to Him, along with the Herodians. . . . [They said to Yeshua], "Tell us then, what do You think? Is it lawful to give a poll-tax to Caesar, or not?" (Matt. 22:15–17 NASB)

We learn much by reading about the makeup of this group. These particular Pharisees were politically allied with King Herod Antipas, an enemy of Yeshua. Therefore, the motivation of this group does not surprise us. They did not ask the question in order to genuinely seek the rabbi's answer, but to trap Yeshua into saying something that would be viewed as negative to his image and reputation. He could not answer the question without being accused of some type of an anti-Jewish position.

John 11:46 ff. is a crucial passage for understanding Pharisaic opposition of a political nature:

> The chief priests and the Pharisees convened a council [of the Sanhedrin], and were saying, "What are we doing? For this man [Yeshua] is performing many signs. If we let Him go on like this, all men will believe in Him, and the Romans will come and take away both our place and our nation." (vv. 47–48 NASB)

These Pharisees had accepted the fact of harsh Roman occupation. However, they were afraid of a Roman reprisal against a religious or grass-roots movement. This fear motivated their relations with Yeshua. The Sadducees also had similar reasons for their political fears, which will be explained later in this chapter.

We see that the Pharisees who opposed Yeshua in the harshest manner did so out of fear of Roman reprisals, and out of their political leanings. Those Pharisees who differed with Yeshua on Torah interpretations are not pictured as his fierce enemies. Such differences of Torah interpretation were quite normal for this period in Israel. Additionally, it is possible that some of these Pharisees belonged to both groups, and opposed Yeshua on the grounds of political opposition *and* Torah interpretation. It cannot be proven conclusively that the Pharisees of *Beyt Hillel* were more sympathetic to Yeshua, and those of *Beyt Shammai* expressed political opposition to Yeshua, but the evidence that exists points in that direction.

The Reaction of the Priests

The New Testament paints a very spotty picture of the overall reaction of the priests to the Messianic movement. The great majority of priests are not shown as reacting either favorably or unfavorably. Rather, the New Testament focuses on the reaction of the family of the High Priest. Additionally, there is at least one New Testament proof of priests becoming Messianic Jews.

> The number of *talmidim* in Yerushalayim [Jerusalem] increased rapidly, and a large crowd of *cohanim* [priests] were becoming obedient to the faith. (Acts 6:7)

The makeup of this crowd is unclear. We simply do not know to what extent there was a favorable reaction to Messianic Judaism among the descendants of Aaron. However, we can be assured, according to the evidence of Acts 6:7, that a following existed among the priests.

There is a vivid picture, however, of the High Priest's family and the priestly Temple authorities reacting negatively to Yeshua and to Messianic Judaism. This negative reaction was political, not doctrinally based.[9] (See Matt. 20:18; 21:15–16, 23, 43–45; 26:3, 14, 47, 59, 65; 27:1–2, 12, 20; 28:11 ff.; Acts 4:1 ff.; 5:4; 7:1 ff.; 9:1 ff., and others).

In all of the these Scriptures, one sees no genuine dialogue regarding doctrinal differences with Yeshua and with Messianic Jews, as one can see in the Yeshua-Pharisee discussions. Instead, action to stop Yeshua's influence was taken by the priestly officials on a number of occasions (see Matt. 21:45–46; 26:3–4; and especially John 11:46–52; Mark 11:18; Acts 5:17).

An examination of these Scriptures reveals that Yeshua's presence was thought of as a threat to the ruling Temple establishment (the High Priest and his family, Temple officials). During Yeshua's lifetime and during the initial growth of Messianic Judaism, there was continual political opposition to Messianic Judaism from this wing of the priests. We do not know whether there were Messianic priests beyond those mentioned in Acts 6:7. The previously mentioned Theophilus may have been one such Messianic priest, but we have no way of knowing for certain.

The Reaction of the Scribes

The scribes were members of an actual profession. This differentiates them from the Pharisees. However, it is likely that many scribes *were* Pharisees. The *Complete Jewish Bible* identifies these scribes as "Torah teachers." Neusner asserted that the scribes were a professional caste of Torah teachers, commentators, interpreters, and lawyers who developed legal theories and taught them to their students. The New Testament singles them out as a separate group, and I will treat them as such in this chapter. Though often allied with the Pharisees, as Neusner noted, "We have no reason to believe that all scribes were Pharisees."[10]

Numerous Scriptures in the *Complete Jewish Bible* refer to the scribes (Matt. 7:29; 12:38; 15:1 ff.; 20:18; 21:15 ff.; 23:13, 15, 23, 25, 27, 29; 27:41; Mark 3:22; 11:18, 27; 12:28; 14:53; John 8:3 ff.; Acts 4:5; 6:12; 23:9). Sometimes the scribes appear to be allies of the priests (see Matt. 20:18; 21:15). At other times, they appear to be allies of the Pharisees (see Matt. 15:1; 23:13). They appear to give nothing but negative input to Yeshua in the above mentioned Scriptures. However, again, the scribes were not one homogeneous group. They were divided as to both doctrinal and political sympathies. Therefore, it is difficult to make one overall statement about their opposition to Yeshua.

Two Scripture passages portray a positive response from the scribes. In Acts 23, we read the account of *Sha'ul's* questioning before the Sanhedrin and the struggle between the Pharisees and the Sadducees. *Sha'ul*, as previously mentioned in this chapter, identified himself as a Pharisee, and stated that he was being interrogated "concerning [his] hope of the resurrection of the dead" (23:6). When this doctrinal point emerged in the interrogation, the Pharisees and Sadducees split over *Sha'ul's* guilt. The scribes sided *with the Pharisees* (and by implication, with *Sha'ul*). Verses 9–10 state:

> So there was a great uproar [over Paul's defense at the interrogation], with some of the *Torah*-teachers [scribes] who were on the side of the *P'rushim* [Pharisees] standing up and joining in— "We don't find anything wrong with this man; and if a spirit or an angel spoke to him, what of it?" The dispute became . . . violent.

Although we cannot be sure that the scribes mentioned here were sympathetic to Paul's Messianic beliefs, they do appear to give him support. Paul and the scribes seem to have shared common beliefs in the resurrection of the dead and in the existence of spiritual beings.

Again, in Mark 12:28–34, one of the scribes asked Yeshua a sincere question regarding the greatest commandment in the Torah. Yeshua's favorable response to him was, "You are not far from the Kingdom of God" (v. 34). Hence, it is evident that there were some sincere reactions to Yeshua among this group.

Another positive response to Yeshua was voiced by some of the scribes present at his discussion with some Sadducees (see Luke 20:39). Whether it meant that these scribes were satisfied that Yeshua silenced some Sadducees or whether it was a sincere sign of sympathy with Yeshua, is not stated. Remember, the scribes, as a whole, were not sympathetic with the belief system of the Sadducees. Luke 20:39 states, "Some of the *Torah*-teachers [scribes] answered [Yeshua], 'Well spoken, Rabbi.'" This followed Yeshua's answer to these Sadducees' trick question regarding the resurrection of the dead. The scribes' reaction, for whatever reason, was sympathetic.

My conclusion is that this professional caste of scribes was primarily opposed to Yeshua and to Messianic Judaism. However, we do not know if some individual scribes became Messianic Jews. We have seen two instances of recorded scribal sympathy toward Yeshua. On some occasions, the scribes are portrayed as allied with the Pharisees; at other times they are shown to be aligned with the Sadducees. The question remains, "How homogeneous was this group of scribes?"

The scribal opposition is sometimes doctrinal, and sometimes political, paralleling the reaction of the Pharisees. There are gaps in our understanding of the exact nature of the scribal reaction. Therefore, I will not draw any additional conclusions.

The Reaction of the Sadducees

The Sadducees, another first-century, Jerusalem-based sect of Judaism, are also shown as having reactions to Yeshua and to Messianic Judaism. The evidence concerning their reactions is minimal, but consistent. Bright noted that the Sadducees were made up of wealthy priests of Jerusalem, "They drew their strength from the priestly aristocracy, and the secular nobility associated with them."[11]

It has not been conclusively proven that all priests of the Jerusalem area belonged to the Sadducee party. Nevertheless, I will treat the Sadducees as a smaller group within the category of the priests. If later scholarship can show that this was not the case, I will gladly accept such findings.

Doctrinally, along with not believing in spirit beings or in the resurrection of the dead, the Sadducees "[gave] authority only to the [written] Torah, and granted [no authority] to the body of oral law developed by the scribes."[12] They focused on the Temple service as the heart of true Judaism.

This sect advocated a strong, continual, sacrificial practice, which was to be carried out by the priesthood. This was central to their hope for the continuation of true Judaism. The Sadducees were rivals to the grass-roots, synagogue-centered, oral-law developing scribes and Pharisees. They believed that their practice of Judaism preserved the heart of the faith.

In Matthew 16:1, some Sadducees (allied here with some Pharisees) came to Galilee and tried to trap Yeshua. We see political opposition, based on something other than doctrinal differences. Yeshua and the Pharisees present actually had more common doctrinal ground than did these Sadducees and these particular Pharisees.

In Matthew 22:23–40, Yeshua confronted these doctrinal differences between himself and some Sadducees. These Sadducees were leading him into a doctrinal trap concerning the resurrection. This conflict was not an actual discussion of doctrine, since both sides held their beliefs quite strongly and were well aware of the leanings of the other side. This was an attempt to silence Yeshua by exposing his illogical thought, but the attempt backfired (see vv. 33–35).

The book of Acts consistently portrays the Sadducees as opposed to the growth of Messianic Judaism. In 4:1–3, the captain of the temple guard arrested John and Peter. This happened because they "were teaching the people the doctrine of resurrection from the dead and offering Yeshua as proof" (v. 2).

We know that the Sadducees strongly opposed the doctrine of resurrection from the dead, as well as any grass-roots movement among the Jewish people that could upset the status quo. They feared a new movement like Messianic Judaism could gain popularity, drawing Roman attention.

Much of the Sadducees' ability to function as they did depended upon their political capitulation to the Roman and Herodian authorities. The reasons behind their opposition to the spread of Messianic Judaism are logical and understandable. Cooperation with Roman authorities existed among the Sadducees. As Bright noted:

> Being practical men . . . they were willing to go to considerable lengths of compromise, readily cooperating with the secular rulers, whether . . . king-priests or Roman procurators . . . fearing above all things any disturbance that might upset the balance. For them . . . the future of Judaism was . . . as a cult community under the Pentateuchal law.[13]

By using the phrase "cult community," Bright was referring to the Temple as the center of Sadducean life. In Acts 5:17–18, again, the High Priest and some Sadducees arrested some Messianic Jews. The text states that these religious officials were "filled with jealousy" (17b). As this movement was gaining members among the people (see 5:14–15; 4:4, 32–35), again, its potential to upset the political status quo threatened the Sadducees.

Returning to a previously cited passage, Acts 23:1–10, we see the Sadducees in opposition to both *Sha'ul* and the Pharisees. Again, this makes sense, given the great fear this popular new movement caused in the Sadducees. Add to this fear, the doctrines of Messianic Judaism, which allied it with the Pharisees, and it is understandable that the Sadducees would have had a negative reaction to any spreading of this faith.

Conclusion

Although evidence is not plentiful, I conclude that the prejudice that stereotypes the Jerusalem religious leaders as having totally rejected Yeshua and Messianic Judaism is *not* accurate. We have seen how various Pharisees and priests became Messianic Jews. We have noted some sympathetic reactions by religious authorities that showed tolerance (such as that of *Rabban Gamliel*).

From the evidence, we can assume that most of the Pharisees, priests, scribes, and Sadducees, reacted negatively to Messianic Judaism. Yet, we cannot over-generalize concerning these groups, as if everyone reacted in the same way. The evidence concerning this matter points to the fact that all religious sects and parties in Jerusalem did not universally oppose Yeshua. When he was opposed, the opposition focused on the issue of whose authority he followed in interpreting the Torah, not whether he kept the Torah. Therefore, we can conclude that the recorded opposition to Yeshua does not change our Torah-observant picture of him.

CHAPTER ELEVEN

THE BOOK
OF ACTS
AND BEYOND

The Early Years

It is worthwhile to examine the reasons why there was opposition to the Messianic Jewish community. If breaking the Torah or the *mitzvot* was a main reason for antagonism against the movement, we should expect to see this recorded in the New Testament. If no such opposition is recorded, it will help to prove the main thrust of this book. The table below will show the reasons given for various persecutions in the inaugural years of the movement.

Recorded Opposition in the Book of Acts

Text	Source of Opposition	Reasons Given
Acts 4:1–4	priests, Temple guard, Sadducees	doctrine of resurrection
Acts 4:5–22	elders, teachers, the High Priest Yosef (Caiaphas), John, Alexander	to prevent spread of doctrine teaching Yeshua as Messiah
Acts 5:17 ff.	high priest, Sadducees	jealousy, fear
Acts 6:8 ff.	synagogue of the Freedmen	false charges of Torah-breaking
Acts 8:3; 9:2	*Sha'ul*	no Torah-breaking charge
Acts 9:23	Damascene religious officials	no Torah-breaking charge

Recorded Opposition in the Book of Acts (continued)

Text	Source of Opposition	Reasons Given
Acts 12:1 ff.	the Herodian king	no Torah-breaking charge
Acts 21:27–29	immigrant community from Asia	false beliefs about what *Sha'ul* taught, due to false rumors

This table demonstrates that there was no valid charge of Torah-breaking in any of the above passages. If any type of Torah-breaking had been advocated, either in teaching or lifestyle, we would have read of protests against it. We simply do not see this (outside of one false charge that is not investigated any further according to the text). Whatever reasons are given for the prejudices against the first-century Messianic movement, Torah-breaking was *not* one of them.

These prejudices and persecutions were caused by the political infighting of this era, coupled with the heavy pressure of Roman occupation. I devote a section of chapter 7 of my essay "The Relationship of Yeshua and the First Century CE Messianic Jewish Community to the *Mitzvot* of the Mosaic Covenant: Demonstrating a Torah-observant Lifestyle" to this very point. Therefore, I refer the reader to that work. The Messianic movement had the potential to threaten the status of the Sadducees and other political powerbrokers of this time. This was the main motivation of the persecutions that occurred. We clearly see this in Acts 5:28, where the High Priest *Hananyah* said to the Messianic Jews, "You have filled Jerusalem with your teaching; moreover, you are determined to make us responsible for this man's death." By using the word *us*, the High Priest was referring to either his direct family or the Sadducees. In addition, the desire to preserve the status quo and not upset the Roman goal of the *Pax Romana*[1] was strong. This also helped lead to the previously mentioned persecutions.

There is no internal evidence from the New Testament that any persecutions occurred because of Torah-breaking. This, in and of itself, tells us much about the type of Torah observance practiced by the early Messianic Jewish community.

The Early Church Fathers

A number of early church fathers commented on the Torah observance of Messianic Jews. Their comments were primarily negative. They could not see the validity of Torah observance. However, their comments show us that Torah observance was flourishing within the early Messianic Jewish communities. For that purpose, it is worthwhile to look at some of their comments.

Ignatius of Antioch (d. 107 C.E.), the early Church authority, encountered Messianic Jews who continued to be Torah-observant. He did not regard their Torah observance as something positive. Concerning some Messianic Jews, he stated, "We have seen how former adherents of the ancient customs have since attained to a new hope, so that they have given up keeping the Sabbath [on Saturday], and now order their lives by the Lord's Day instead [Sunday]." In his Epistle to the Magnesians, Ignatius wrote, "To profess Jesus Christ while continuing to follow Jewish customs is an absurdity. The Christian faith does not look to Judaism, but Judaism looks to Christianity" (1:11).[2]

Although Ignatius did not live in Israel and was not able to see the Messianic lifestyle there, he did have opportunities to observe Messianic Jews from Antioch to Philippi, where he had journeyed. His attitude was remarkably different from that of *Rav Sha'ul*, who traversed the same geographical area some forty years before Ignatius. In general, his letter to the Magnesians opposed the practices of the Torah, yet his opposition indicates that Torah-observant Jews existed in Asia Minor at about the year 100 C.E.

The church father, Justin (late second century), described Messianic Jews who kept the Torah. Some tried to persuade Gentile believers to do the same, while others did not.

Pritz noted that the church father, Epiphanius (late fourth century), knew of Messianic Jews whose Torah observance divided them from the mainstream of non-Jewish believers in Jesus. "It is their observance of the Law [i.e., the Torah] and this alone which for Epiphanius separates the Nazarenes from the main Church."[3] Epiphanius described these Messianic Jews in the following manner:

> Jews [who] dedicate themselves to the Law and submit to circumcision. . . . They remained wholly Jewish . . . they use not only the New Testament, but also the Old, like [all of] the Jews . . . [they] live according to the preaching of the Law as among Jews. They do not agree with the Christians because they are trained in the Law [i.e., Torah], in circumcision, the Sabbath and the other things.[4]

The early church father, Eusebius, provided an important witness of Torah-observant Messianic Judaism as being the norm in the first century C.E. "The apostolic men of his [*Shim'on*'s] day, who it seems were of the Hebrew stock and therefore, in the Jewish manner, still retained most of their ancient customs."[5] He further described first-century Messianic Jews in these words, "They observed the Sabbath [on Saturday] and the whole Jewish [halakhic and legal] system."[6]

In Ignatius' view, Messianic Jews were not to be regarded as Jewish. Additionally, he felt that it was wrong for them to continue in their Jewish lifestyle. Interestingly, no record exists in the New Testament of Messianic Jews not being considered Jews due to their belief in Yeshua as the Messiah. Indeed, Professor Lawrence Schiffman indicated that this would have been a halakhic impossibility at that time. According to his findings, there was nothing the first Messianic Jews could do or believe that would disqualify them from being Jews.[7] If Schiffman was accurate, with no danger of losing their Jewish status, we would expect the Messianic community to continue to keep their Jewish lifestyle and customs, based on God's revelation through the Torah.

Tomson summed up the opinion of the early church fathers toward Messianic Torah observance by stating, "The apostolic fathers were of the opinion . . . that the Jewish Apostles naturally observed the [Torah] commandments."[8] In spite of the negative attitude that prevailed among the early church fathers toward Judaism and Messianic Jews, there is evidence from their writings that Messianic Jews continued to be Torah-observant. This fact adds to our perception of Torah observance as the norm for early Messianic Jews.

PART FOUR

TORAH
OBSERVANCE:
LEGALISM
OR LOVE?

CHAPTER TWELVE

LOVE, GRACE, AND MERCY IN THE FIRST MESSIANIC COMMUNITY

It has been clearly demonstrated that Yeshua and the first-generation of Messianic Jews were Torah-observant. They lived their lives guided by the *mitzvot* of the Torah. Yet, it is extremely important for us to observe *the manner in which* they kept the Torah. Namely, what was the role of love, grace, and mercy in their Torah observance? Did the first Messianic Jewish communities keep the Torah in a pushy, legalistic manner? Did they attempt to prove anything by their keeping of the Torah? In this chapter, we will look at the attitude with which the first Messianic Jews observed the Torah.

First, let me explain my use of the word *love* in describing Torah observance. By this, I do not use a contemporary definition where love is an intense emotional feeling. Instead, I prefer to look at love in light of the Torah. In Leviticus 19:18b, it is written, "Love your neighbor as yourself" (Hebrew, ואהבת לרעך כמוך, *v'ahavta l'reyekhah k'mokha*). Often, the Torah explains itself by giving examples of concepts such as love. If we look at how people are to treat each other according to the Torah, we have a practical definition of the Hebrew word *ahava* (love). To briefly summarize what the Torah describes in great length, to love means to *care for the welfare of your neighbor*. The word used for *neighbor* in biblical Hebrew means *friend*. When I ask if the first Messianic Jews kept the Torah with love, I am asking if the Messianic community cared for people with their true welfare in mind. Did they relate to others, and to their own, as friends? This definition will be kept in mind as we look at this question.

In addition, we must define the word "grace" as I use it above. Did the Messianic community observe the Torah in a grace-full manner? By using the word *grace*, I am asking if their Torah observance reflected the true personality of God, or did it pervert the character of God, who revealed himself to *Moshe* as a God of grace (see Exod. 20:6; 34:6; Num. 14:18)? Did their keeping of the *mitzvot* help to bring people closer to God? The Hebrew concept of grace is most clearly reflected in a two-word Hebrew phrase, חן וחסד *hen v'chesed*. This phrase may best be translated as "grace that is tied to a covenant." The true definition of grace, then, is one that is based on the covenants that we have received from God. These are the covenants to Abraham, Isaac, and Jacob. *Shim'on* showed how important the covenants were to his faith when he described God as "The God of Abraham, Isaac and Jacob, the God of our fathers." (Acts 3:13). He directly tied in the covenants made with the Fathers to the promise of Yeshua's salvation, which he spoke about in this same verse. We will be looking for evidence to see if the Messianic community kept the Torah in a way that reflected God's covenant love and faithfulness.

Finally, by using the term *mercy*, I am asking if the Messianic community kept the Torah by doing good deeds and compassionately relating to those in need. The Hebrew concept often rendered into English as *mercy* is the word רחמים, *rachamim*.[1] The word *rachamim* conveys a wonderful word picture in biblical Hebrew. The Hebrew word for womb comes from the same root as *mercy—rachamim*. The concept of mercy reflects the loving care and nourishment that a mother gives to her unborn fetus, leading to its ultimate birth. A beautiful picture of this sort of tender mercy is provided in Isaiah 49:15.

> "Can a woman forget her nursing child, And have no compassion on the sons of her womb? Even these may forget, but I will not forget you!" (NASB)

In this verse, the Hebrew word מרחם, *m'rachem* is used for *compassion*. It comes from the same root as the word for a womb, and is one of the present tense verb forms for the noun *rachamim*.

Did the Torah observance of the early Messianic Jews cause the doing of good deeds and the performance of merciful acts? Did it reflect this merciful side of God, these "womb" mercies? These are questions that we will seek to answer in this chapter. There is no clear and easy division between these three concepts. Love, grace, and mercy are all tied closely together in the Torah, both as concepts and, more importantly, as practical actions.

Luke Writes to Theophilus

The book of Acts gives us the best opportunity to see the daily lifestyle of the first Messianic Jewish community (in Jerusalem). Acts is the historical record of the development of both the Messianic Jewish movement and of the spread of belief in Yeshua among non-Jewish peoples. Therefore, it becomes the crucial text for us in understanding how the early

Messianic Jewish community kept the Torah. Remember also, that the person receiving both the gospel of Luke and the book of Acts, Theophilus, would have paid strict attention to how the first Messianic Jews related to the Torah.[2]

As a priest (probably a Sadducee), and a possible relative of the High Priest, Theophilus would have had a negative reaction to any demonstration of Torah ignorance by the first Messianic Jewish community of Jerusalem. Luke presented the Messianic movement to Theophilus as one that carried out the *mitzvot* of the Torah in love.

Luke and Acts should be best understood as a pair of books written by Luke to Theophilus. The two books form a whole, with one author and one purpose: to explain the Messianic movement's beliefs and history to Theophilus. As Luke put it, "I, too, should write you an accurate . . . narrative, so that you might know how well-founded are the things about which you have been taught" (Luke 1:3b–4).

Luke presented Yeshua as part of a lineage of good, Torah-observant Jews. In the ancient Middle East, particularly in Jewish society, one's family lineage was an extremely important aspect of an individual's identity. If a family was known for its devout Torah observance, then it was considered to be of good quality. Theophilus would only have considered the Messiahship of Yeshua as a possibility if Yeshua came from a devout, Torah-observant family with a connection to King David. This was a crucial point!

In the 21st century Western world, this concern with lineage may seem foreign to us. However, even today, these considerations are prevalent in the Middle East, and among many Jewish communities worldwide. If Luke could present Yeshua's family as devout and Torah-observant, Theophilus would be favorably impressed. Proving that there was a connection to the priesthood in Yeshua's bloodline would have lessened any hostility Theophilus may have felt toward Yeshua's beliefs. Luke is careful to point out to Theophilus that many priests had become Messianic Jews (Acts 6:7).

Luke showed Theophilus that Yeshua had a devout family lineage with roots from King David (see Luke 3:31) and from Judah (see v. 33). The connection to King David was important because the Messiah was believed to be a descendant of King David by all Jews. Therefore, the genealogy (chapter 3) was an important part of Luke's message to Theophilus. To a modern-day Western reader, this genealogy may seem boring and irrelevant. Nothing could be further from the truth! This genealogy was purposely placed in the beginning of the book for Theophilus to examine. It was an important part of Luke's picture of Yeshua. For our purposes, it also helps to establish the fact that the first Messianic community valued Torah observance. One of its spokesmen, Luke, presented the Messiah as Torah-observant, using his genealogy as partial proof of this fact.

An Example from the First Messianic Community

Let us examine the evidence of love in the first Messianic community. As defined above, love means *caring for the welfare of one's neighbor.* Given that the first Messianic community was Torah-observant, evidences of their active love will help us see how they kept the Torah.

> All those trusting in Yeshua stayed together and had everything in common; in fact, they sold their property and possessions and distributed the proceeds to all who were in need. Continuing faithfully . . . to meet in the Temple courts daily, and breaking bread in their several homes, they shared their food in joy and simplicity of heart, praising God and having the respect of all the people. (Acts 2:44–47)

> And the congregation of those who believed were of one heart and soul; and not one of them claimed that anything belonging to him was his own, but all things were common property to them. (Acts 4:32)

It is evident that caring for one's neighbor was a top priority in the young Messianic movement. Three separate community actions are mentioned here: having all possessions in common, selling property and possessions and giving the money from the sales to the needy, and sharing meals with others. The effect of living out the concept of love was that the early Messianic Jews had the respect of the entire population of Jerusalem.

Acts 6 further affirms that the first Messianic Jews vigilantly cared for each other.

> Now at this time while the disciples were increasing in number, a complaint arose on the part of the Hellenistic Jews against the native Hebrews, because their widows were being overlooked in the daily serving [food distribution]. (vs. 1 NASB)

Here, we learn that one group of Messianic Jews was being neglected. In the community, this was perceived as a wrong—and this wrong was quickly rectified (see verse 3). By tending to the needs of the widows in their midst, the first Messianic Jewish community was fulfilling the Torah. Caring for widows is a high priority in the Torah (see Exod. 22:22; Deut. 24:17; 26:12; Ps. 23:10; Isa. 1:17). Yeshua's brother James, the chief rabbi of the first Messianic community, summed up the proper attitude, "Pure and undefiled religion in the sight of our God and Father is this: to visit orphans and widows in their distress, and to keep oneself unstained by the world (James 1:27 NASB).

Again, we see the priority given to helping widows. Let me emphasize that *Ya'akov* was saying exactly what is written in the Torah. He was teaching his community to fulfill a *mitzvah*. He would only have done this if he saw it as an important teaching from the Torah.

In Acts 3, we see another example of the early Messianic Jews helping a disadvantaged person in their city. Peter and John healed a handicapped man on the way to the *minchah* (afternoon) service at the Temple (vv. 1–7). Physical healing was a common occurrence for the first Messianic Jews. The benefactors of these healings were citizens from Jerusalem and surrounding areas.

> Also the people from the cities in the vicinity of Jerusalem were coming together, bringing people who were sick or afflicted with unclean spirits; and they were all being healed. (Acts 5:16 NASB)

From this verse, we see that healing flowed from the Messianic community to those in need. The believers followed the example of Yeshua by giving as he gave.

In Acts 5, *Rabban Gamliel* makes an interesting comment. *Rabban Gamliel* was considered a great sage in Judaism. He was a Pharisee, and was renowned for his fervent and compassionate Torah observance. According to the Talmud:

> When Rabban Gamliel died, the glory of the Torah ceased, and purity and abstinence died. (*Sotah* 9:15)

His proposition to the Jerusalem Sanhedrin—that time would tell if Messianic Judaism was a movement that was initiated by God or by man—is recorded in Acts 5:38–39.

> In the present case [of the Messianic Jews], I say to you, stay away from these men and let them alone, for if this plan or action is of men, it will be overthrown; but if it is of God, you will not be able to overthrow them; or else you may even be found fighting against God. (NASB)

It is interesting that *Rabban Gamliel* never once leveled a charge of Torah-breaking against Messianic Jews. We should expect that such a devout teacher of the Torah would have done so if there had been any validity to this charge, but he wisely left room for the movement to prove itself. I can only surmise that a major way in which *Rabban Gamliel* would have judged the validity of Messianic Judaism was by observing whether the community kept the Torah mercifully and without using violence as a means of reaching their goals. (See Acts 5:36–37, where *Gamliel* judges the violent [yet Torah-following] movements of Theudas and Judah to have not been by God's initiation.)

Further proof of the merciful, loving way in which the Torah was kept by the fledgling movement is shown in Acts 8. There, an immigrant Greek-speaking Messianic Jew, Philip (see Acts 6:5) traveled to Samaria to teach that Yeshua was the promised Messiah. This was in accordance with instructions given to Yeshua's students in Acts 1:8, " '. . . you will be my witnesses both in Yerushalayim [Jerusalem] and in all Y'hudah [Judah] and Shomron [Samaria], indeed to the ends of the earth!' " The result of Philip's ministry to the people was that ". . . there was great joy in that city [Samaria]" (Acts 8:8). The text tells of Philip's teaching, performance of signs and wonders, physical healings, and freeing people of demonic spirits. Such actions, along with their results, can only be looked upon as a loving, merciful demonstration of God's presence.

Another touching event took place in the early history of Messianic Judaism. It also displayed a merciful approach to keeping the Torah. *Shim'on* brought a dead woman to life. This is a very similar act to that of the prophet Elisha (see 2 Kings 4:32–37). Elisha was devoutly Torah-observant. His actions and deeds flowed from his faith in the God of Israel. We should see *Shim'on*'s actions and deeds, as recorded here in Acts 9, as proceeding from the same source and motivation as those of Elisha.

Acts 11:27–30 provides another example of the spirit with which the early Messianic Jews kept the Torah.

> During this time, some prophets came down from Yerushalayim [Jerusalem] to Antioch; and one of them named Agav [Agabus] stood up and through the Spirit predicted that there was going to be a severe famine throughout the Roman Empire. (It took place while Claudius was Emperor.) So the *talmidim* decided to provide relief to the brothers living in Y'hudah [Judah], each according to his means; and they did it, sending their contribution to the elders in the care of Bar-Nabba [Barnabbas] and *Sha'ul*.

Here, the Messianic Jews in Antioch probably sent a monetary contribution to their fellow Messianic Jews in Judah, due to the beginning of a great famine. Barnabas and *Rav Sha'ul* took their contribution to Judah's Messianic leaders.

Love, care, and concern for the welfare of Judah's Messianic community were foremost in the heart of Antioch's Messianic community. They cared for the welfare of their fellow Messianic Jews, although few, if any, of them had ever met any members of Jerusalem's Messianic community. Their giving was a sign of love for their fellow community members, and was given in the hope of relieving them of suffering. This incident demonstrates that early Messianic Jews saw love as a crucial part of keeping the Torah.

Volumes have not been written on this subject. However, the previously mentioned Acts 6 narrative, combined with this Acts 11 narrative, affirms that Messianic Jews, both in Israel and in the Diaspora, cared for the welfare of their fellow Messianic Jews, regardless of whether they were known to them in person.

CHAPTER THIRTEEN

A SIGN OF LOVE TO THE NATIONS

Perhaps the biggest example of the early Messianic Jews keeping the Torah in a merciful, loving way came as a surprise. This involved the opening up of the kingdom of God to non-Jews.

In the world of the first century, non-Jews could be part of the Jewish community by belonging to one of at least two categories of persons: the Godfearer (see chapter 5), or the full convert (Hebrew, גר צדק, *ger tzedek*). Other categories of non-Jews also existed and it would take a whole book to adequately explain all of them. Nevertheless, the idea was that a non-Jew could embrace the God of Israel by believing in one God and then undergoing circumcision, with a commitment to living as a Jew (keeping the Torah, including the Jewish calendar cycle). Such a person was a *ger tzedek* and was considered fully Jewish. A significant number of Messianic Jews were of the opinion that, in order to believe in Yeshua, a non-Jew would have to undergo conversion and become a *ger tzedek*, and from there embrace Yeshua as the Messiah. This category of Messianic Jews is described in the book of Acts (15:1, 5).

According to Acts 15:2, the question that urgently needed a halakhic ruling was, "What should be required of non-Jews in order for them to take part in the Messianic Jewish movement?" That is, what do Gentiles need to do in order to believe in Yeshua as the Messiah, and in the God of Israel? Should they be made to undergo full conversion to become a *ger tzedek*? Should they be required to become *gerey hasha'ar* and embrace just the Noachide commandments, the Sabbath, kosher dietary laws, and maintain regular synagogue attendance?[1] If not, what should be required of them? This was a bold inquiry, and we should respect the courage and integrity of the Messianic Jewish rabbis' council that took part in the halakhic decision of Acts 15.

Too many Bible teachers have reproved the first-century Jewish people for hardness of heart—but here is a situation where Jews made a halakhic decision to open the kingdom of God to non-Jews. The Messianic leaders had love for non-Jews, whom they heard were embracing belief in the one God of Israel and in Yeshua as the Messiah. The welfare of these new Gentile believers in Yeshua was of great importance to these Messianic Jewish leaders. Their halakhic ruling was in accordance with *Ya'akov*'s statement.

> James answered, saying, "Brethren, listen to me. Simeon [*Shim'on*] has related how God first concerned Himself about taking from among the Gentiles a people for His name. With this the words of the Prophets agree, just as it is written, 'After these things I will return, and I will rebuild the tabernacle of David which has fallen, and I will rebuild its ruins, and I will restore it, so that the rest of mankind may seek the LORD, and all the Gentiles who are called by My name,' says the LORD, who makes these things known from long ago. Therefore it is my judgment that we do not trouble those who are turning to God from among the Gentiles, but that we write to them that they abstain from things contaminated by idols and from fornication and from what is strangled and from blood." (Acts 15:13–20 NASB)

James was in the position to issue the summary statement, the halakhic ruling. He occupied the position of chief rabbi of the Jerusalem Messianic community. I have discussed his position in a previous portion of this book. By this statement, these courageous Messianic Jews opened the kingdom of God to all who would believe in Yeshua, regardless of ethnic background.

Shim'on served as a spokesman for the halakhic decision that was made (see Acts 15:7–11), and he became God's first emissary to Gentiles mentioned in the New Testament. *Shim'on* was God's instrument for opening God's kingdom to non-Jews, as were *Sha'ul*, Barnabas, and many others.

According to this decision, four things were prohibited to the new Gentile believers in Messiah Yeshua. The prohibitions (see Acts 15:20) concerned idolatry, fornication, eating strangled animals, and blood (either eating or shedding blood). One or both of the last prohibitions deals with kosher dietary laws, and possibly, one deals with murder. These prohibitions concerned matters of the Torah, as well as issues that could destroy fellowship between non-Jewish believers in Yeshua and Messianic Jews. Idolatry, sexual sins, basic kosher dietary laws, and murder were such crucial Torah-related issues that the halakhic decision required Gentiles to keep the Torah on these four points. Not to do so would have constituted a break in fellowship with both God and the mother Messianic Jewish community.

For Gentiles in the category of Godfearers, this would not have been difficult, since they already were keeping these four Torah *mitzvot*, and many, many more. A Gentile from a pagan, Hellenistic background, however, would have needed some re-education to understand the significance of these matters. *Sha'ul* and the Messianic Jewish emissaries would have given such an education to new Gentile believers when they taught in their congregations.

To summarize, Acts 15 demonstrates that through their halakhic decision, the Messianic Jewish leadership in Israel very much loved and cared for the new, believing Gentile world. In addition, their decision showed their love for their own Messianic Jewish community. The leaders considered the needs and situation of both groups in forming their *halakhah*. In keeping the Torah, the Messianic Jewish leaders loved their fellow man. Rabbi *Sha'ul* stated it well:

> Don't owe anyone anything—except to love one another; for whoever loves his fellow human being has fulfilled *Torah*. . . . Love does not do harm to a neighbor; therefore love is the fullness of *Torah*. (Rom. 13:8, 10)

There should be no doubt that the early Messianic Jews, beginning with the Jerusalem leadership, kept the Torah—with love as their motivation. In addition, we have seen this love manifested through good deeds and healings. The early Messianic Jews showed God's mercy to others. This is especially true in the opening of the kingdom of God to Gentiles, as narrated in Acts 15.

As to the question of whether the expression of compassion through such deeds brought the recipient closer to God, let us look at the following chart. Here, I cite the reactions of the recipients to the aforementioned acts of love.

Reactions to God's Workings

Text	Action	Reaction
Acts 3:1–11	Healing	Walking and praising God (vv. 8–9)
Acts 8:5–8, 14	Healings, freedom from demonic spirits, receiving the Word of God	There was great joy.

Reactions to God's Workings (continued)

Text	Action	Reaction
Acts 8:26–40	Explaining of the Prophets, immersion in a *mikvah*,[2]	He continued on his way, full of joy.
Acts 10:1–48	Explaining of who Messiah is to Godfearers, receiving of God's Spirit	Embracing the God of Israel
Acts 13:15–49	Explaining who Messiah is to Jews and non-Jews	Some embrace Messiah.

In these few texts, we see the recipients turning toward God. Whether they verbally praised God, repented, and trusted in Messiah Yeshua—or were just full of joy because of God's mercy—their reaction demonstrates movement toward God. Messianic Jews caused a turning to God on behalf of the recipient of the actions.

Had *Shim'on* thought that God was merely telling him to stop keeping the Torah's dietary laws (see chapter 6), then many Gentiles in Caesarea would not have received the message about Yeshua. *Shim'on* was obedient to God's will as revealed in the vision, and because of this the kingdom was opened to the Gentiles.

CHAPTER FOURTEEN

THE TORAH ON HOW TO OBSERVE THE TORAH

We have seen several passages from the book of Acts, which demonstrate that the Messianic Jewish community kept the Torah with love, grace, and mercy. This fact should not surprise us. The Torah affirms the type of attitude that God wanted the Jewish people to have concerning its observance.

> "And you shall love the LORD your God with all your heart and with all your soul and with all your might. And these words, which I am commanding you today, shall be on your heart; and you shall teach them diligently to your sons and shall talk of them when you sit in your house and when you walk by the way and when you lie down and when you rise up." (Deut. 6:5–7 NASB)

All Israel—through all its generations—is instructed to love God by internalizing the Torah, and teaching it at all times and in all situations in life.[1] The Messianic community kept the Torah as an expression of their love for God. They considered it God's gift of mercy and grace. By providing healing through the power of their faith in Yeshua the Messiah—they were keeping the Torah in love. By giving monetary gifts to the hunger-stricken Messianic Jews in Israel—they were keeping the Torah in love. Whatever the action, it was done with the compassion that flowed from Yeshua to the individual or the community, in order to live out the words of the Torah. This is the attitude and motivation described in Deuteronomy 6.

I do not mean to glorify or idolize the Torah, if that were possible. It is not God. God alone is God; but his will, his ways, and the very promises of the coming of the Messiah are all revealed in the Torah. To know and love the Torah is to know God better, and to better love him on his terms. If we look at Deuteronomy 6:5–7 with the above in mind, we can understand why learning and practicing the Torah is so crucial for our lives. This is true for both Messianic Jews and Gentiles who believe in the Jewish Messiah, Yeshua. As it is written:

> Teach me Thy statutes.
> Make me understand the way of Thy precepts,
> So I will meditate on Thy wonders. (Ps. 119:26b–27 NASB)

From my experience in Israel as a Messianic Jewish leader, I am familiar with the kinds of responses toward Torah observance that may occur. Some may be fearful of doing anything connected with the Torah and Jewish tradition. Others may be so devoted to keeping the *mitzvot* in a specific manner, that unhealthy attitudes develop, such as pride, one-upmanship, and losing sight of the mercy and grace of God.

While in Israel, I participated in a study group that, for three years, examined the relationship between the *mitzvot* and the New Testament. We sought ways in which to apply the findings to our own lives. Our conclusion, ever resounding in my ears today, was to allow each family the freedom to decide how to keep the *mitzvot* in their lives. No pressure to conform—to keep the *mitzvot* in a certain way—would be placed upon anyone. We aspired to educate ourselves in order to make knowledgeable and responsible decisions regarding our lifestyles and the keeping of the *mitzvot*.

Now, years later, I look back upon that conclusion and believe it to be the best starting point with which to embark upon a modern, Torah-observant Messianic Judaism. We can help each other learn the Torah, and understand the principles by which Yeshua lived out the *mitzvot*. At the same time, we should not push each other to be conformed to our own standards. When Messiah returns, he will ultimately teach us the perfect way to keep the *mitzvot* in the mercy and love of God. Until then, as the Torah-observant Messianic rabbi, *Sha'ul* of Tarsus, stated, "We see through a dirty mirror" (1 Cor. 13:12, author's translation). In other words, we struggle with what knowledge and love we have, in order to do our best to live correctly. This is not reneging on our responsibility to observe the Torah. We will differ in our interpretation of how to observe it. This is to be expected. We have seen that it was normative throughout Jewish history. Whatever differences we may have with other communities are probably healthy ones. We should not feel pressured or pressure others to quickly change.

The prophet Micah spoke about the proper and loving way in which the Torah was meant to be kept:

> He has told you, O man, what is good;
> And what does the LORD require of you
> But to do justice, to love kindness,
> And to walk humbly with your God? (Mic. 6:8 NASB)

The New Testament portrays the Messianic community as keeping the Torah according to the words of Micah. Justice, covenant love, and humility were to be the trademarks of a man who kept it. This first-century community kept the Torah in the way prescribed by God himself—with the right heart attitude. May our observance of it honor God in the same way!

CONCLUSION

The evidence clearly confirms that the individuals studied in this book, including Yeshua himself, lived a Torah-observant lifestyle. Though the exact methods of Torah observance may have differed between people—the Torah was not discarded as an invalid document. Their continued observance of the Torah implies its ongoing significance in their lives and their acceptance of this theological fact.

Throughout the regions of Jewish settlement, and within different religious movements of this time, various emphases and halakhic standards existed. This is reflected in the lives of Messianic Jews, as well as in the lives of all of Israel's population. There was no universally accepted understanding of the manner in which to observe the Torah. In some sense, this fact parallels the approach to the Torah of Jewry today.

Yet, the Torah was, in one way or another, observed by the first-century Messianic Jewish movement. Some of these people had a pro-Pharisaic understanding of Torah observance, possibly allying themselves with followers of Hillel. Rabbi Harvey Falk argued for such an understanding in his work *Jesus the Pharisee*. It appears that *Sha'ul* was this type of Messianic Jew. Others in the Messianic community would have approached the Torah with a more regionalized understanding.

Since the historical data confirms a Torah-observant first-century Messianic Judaism, how can we use this conclusion to inform our practice today? I have no easy answers, but I do have some observations. These are passionately felt observations, built on both my reading of history and my own experience over the past twenty-eight years.

It behooves followers of Messiah to develop a theology that is true to the pattern of observance found in the Scriptures. While doing so, care must be taken to fulfill the *mitzvot* in a merciful manner, without placing pressure on others to do as we do. Therefore, speaking, as one who believes in a merciful, grace-filled, and Torah-observant Messianic Judaism, I urge a closer study of Yeshua's practice of Torah observance. He is the perfect role model.

May we who follow Messiah in this way do so with mercy and love as our guide. Consequently, our observance of the Torah will be a blessing to the memory of Yeshua, as well as serve to bring our friends and loved ones to the knowledge of God. Additionally, those of us in the Messianic Jewish community need to exhibit love and acceptance to non-Jewish believers in Yeshua. Whatever we decide our calling and special purposes are as Messianic Jews, we should never consider ourselves better or more loved by God due to our bloodline. We are not better, nor more loved. As

Jews, we do have a special calling, function, and role (see Exod. 19: 5–6). Yet, together with Gentile believers, we are part of the redeemed people of God worldwide, throughout the history of mankind. May our words and actions reflect these truths.

EPILOGUE

Messianic Jews in the Future

Only a few passages of Scripture speak of Messianic Jewish communities in the future. However, it is worthwhile to examine any indications of Torah observance.

Revelation 12:17 describes persecution against the "children of the woman."

> The dragon was infuriated over the woman and went off to fight the rest of her children, those who obey God's commands and bear witness to Yeshua.

These children are identified as those who των τηρουντων τας εντολας του θεου και εχοντων την μαρτυριαν Ιησου (Greek, *ton terounton tas entolas tou Theou kai echonton ten marturian Iesou*). This verse speaks of the "ones who keep the commandments of God" and "testify concerning Yeshua." As was previously noted, the word used for *commandments* (*entolas*) is often used as the Greek cognate word for *mitzvah*. Therefore, it appears that the evil power in Revelation 12 seeks to destroy Messianic Jews who are observing the *mitzvot*. No group meets these criteria better than the Messianic Jewish community. First, these are people who obey God's commands. Second, these people bear witness to Yeshua's identity.

Millennial-age texts also give evidence as to future Messianic Jewish Torah observance.

> "In those days ten men from all the nations will grasp [the corner of] the garment of a Jew, saying, 'Let us go with you, for we have heard that God is with you.'" (Zech. 8:23 NASB)

What was on the corner of a garment of a Jew of Zechariah's day? In fulfillment of the *mitzvah*, there were fringes. Numbers 15:37–40 describes this *mitzvah*:

> "Tell them that they shall make for themselves tassels [fringes/ *tzitziyot*] on the corners of their garments throughout their generations . . . to look at and remember all the commandments of the Lord." (vv. 38–39)

Here is a picture of Messianic Jews in the millennial age keeping the *mitzvah* of wearing fringes. Men from the nations (Gentiles) will want to learn from them.

In addition, the prophet Zechariah described a day in which *all* the nations of the world will come to the pilgrimage festival of *Sukkot* in Jerusalem, to observe the festival and worship God. Certainly, the Jewish nation would be present for this occasion, as recorded in Zechariah 14:16–21.

> Then it will come about that any who are left of all the nations that went against Jerusalem will go up from year to year to worship the King, the Lord of hosts, and to celebrate the Feast of Booths. (v. 16)

The celebration of the Feast of Booths is a *mitzvah* from the Torah. Therefore, that Yeshua and the first Messianic Jewish community kept *Sukkot* should not surprise us. The pattern is there, even for the future.

Very few portions of the Torah are dedicated to illustrating a picture of the Messianic Jewish community in the future, so we cannot draw many conclusions. However, it is noteworthy that Zechariah provides us with a picture of Torah-observant Messianic Jews in the millennial age.

ENDNOTES

Chapter One

[1] With the particular group of Pharisees and other Torah-observant teachers whom Yeshua castigated in Matthew 23:5–7, it is the issue of their practice *not* paralleling their teaching that angers him. Their lives were not an integrated whole.

[2] The Talmud contains examples of non-Jews discussing learning the Torah and conversion with both Hillel and Shammai. These discussions appear to have been short and to the point, especially with Shammai.

[3] Falk 21.

Chapter Two

[1] See Hagner 95, for his summary of scholarly Jewish positions on this question.

[2] Safrai lecture.

[3] Vermes 23.

[4] *Mishnah Yadayim* 3:5 is another classic example of doctrinal differences having a political source. It states, "Rabbi Yosi says, 'Qohelet [The book of Ecclesiastes] does not render the hands ritually impure; concerning The Song of Songs, there is a difference of opinion.' Rabbi Shimon says, 'Qohelet is one of the leniencies of Bet Shammai, and one of the stringencies of Bet Hillel.' Rabbi Shimon ben 'Azai says, 'I received teaching from the 72 elders . . . that the Song of Songs and Qohelet render the hands ritually impure.'" This *mishnah* portrays a long argument on whether the books of Song of Songs and Ecclesiastes are to be counted as Scripture. The varied viewpoints represent different yeshivas and their leaders' opinions.

[5] Safrai lecture.

[6] Safrai lecture. (Additionally, there is no connection between this Hasidic movement, and the Hasidic movement of today's modern period, which began in Eastern Europe.)

[7] Lachs 72.

[8] In Mark 1:30–31, Yeshua healed *Shim'on*'s mother-in-law on a Sabbath. This incident would not have caused any problem in terms of transportation laws, since she was in bed in her own home. To a follower of *Beyt Shammai*, however, there would have been a legal problem with this healing on the Sabbath, due to *Beyt Shammai*'s interpretation of the Sabbath laws.

[9] Parkes 59, 61.

[10] *Kal vachomer* (Hebrew, "light to heavy") refers to an *a fortiori* argument. According to accepted rabbinic hermeneutics of the Second Temple era, this was one of the main methods to employ to interpret the Torah. Rabbi Hillel, barely

one generation before Yeshua, employed it as one of his seven accepted methods for interpreting the Torah.

[11] *Avot* is Hebrew, referring to the thirty-nine work activities that are forbidden on the Sabbath. Although they were not finalized as a system until over a century after Yeshua's death, the principles were well-developed by the first century C.E.

[12] Safrai lecture.

[13] Dr. Safrai noted that this incident probably took place during the second week of counting the 'Omer, between Passover and the Feast of Weeks. The grain in Israel was not yet ripe, but there is a good possibility that it would have been fit to eat around the Kinneret (Sea of Galilee). Because new grain was not quite ripe around the country, it was easy to be hungry at this time of year. This incident has a very believable halakhic argument that highlights it.

[14] The exact nature of the grain under question in Matthew 12:1–8 is not clear. In my opinion, the best rendition of the text is to say that this incident took place in "an unspecified type of grain field." The grain is called *sporamos* in the text, and is rendered by some scholars (e.g., Stern, Ardent, Gingrich, and Newman) as "wheat." Other scholars (Liddell, Scott, the NIV, and Jerusalem Bible translators) identify *sporamos* as "corn." A study of the Greek and Hebrew words used for these crops does not give us concrete conclusions. I did a study of the words *puron, sitos, stakues,* and *steiron* in the Greek, and of *hitah, bar,* and *shibalim* in the Hebrew, in the hope of clearly identifying this crop. Context would lead me to believe that wheat is being referred to here, since the action depicted in this section (hand rubbing the crop in order to eat it) is more suggestive of eating wheat or barley grain than of eating corn. Additionally, the barley and wheat harvests would have occurred in the Lower Galilee at approximately the time of year, from Passover to the Feast of Weeks, which fits our context. The use of the Septuagint to help decipher the meaning of the New Covenant Greek words used is also not conclusive. The word *sitos* (Greek), used in the Septuagint to denote corn, is used at least twelve times in the New Covenant to clearly denote wheat. Therefore, based on the strength of the context, I am considering this crop to be some type of grain, probably either wheat or barley.

[15] Vermes 24.

[16] See note 10 in this chapter.

[17] Safrai lecture.

[18] See note 11 in this chapter.

[19] John Fischer, "Jesus and Early Judaism," 21.

[20] Safrai lecture.

[21] Vermes 26.

Chapter Three

[1] Safrai and Stern, 746–748.

Chapter Four

[1] Vermes 11.

[2] Vermes 18.

[3] See note 11 in chapter 2.

[4] Bivin and Blizzard 155.

[5] John Fischer, "Jesus and Early Judaism," 23.

[6] *Acharit hayamim* is the Hebrew term employed for the "end of days." It refers to that period during which cataclysmic events will occur, fulfilling the prophecies of the Torah, and during which the Messiah will come and the 1,000 year (millennial) reign will begin.

[7] See Lee's excellent work *The Galilean Jewishness of Jesus*, which agrees with the Torah-observant idea set forth in this book.

[8] That Luke was a "Godfearer" (in the category of *phobomenos*) is considered a real possibility by Dr. Flusser, as reported to me in conversation with the Jerusalem School of Synoptic Research (a think-tank of combined Jewish and Christian scholars) in 1996. Dr. Flusser's opinion on Theophilus' identity was related to me in a lecture given by Dr. Fischer in Minneapolis, Minnesota, in August 1991. Dr. Fischer's conjecture on the identity of Luke was relayed at the same lecture.

[9] Falk 21.

[10] *Shaliach tzibbur* refers to the official who functioned as a public reader of the Torah during Shabbat, often reading sections from the Torah or from the *haftarot* (various readings from the Prophets).

[11] Safrai lecture. (*Tzitzit* are fringes on the corners of a garment, worn by every Jewish male in the time of Yeshua. *T'fillin* are phylacteries, which were also worn by Jewish males in the time of Yeshua. Both of these ritual clothing items are based on the Torah's command to wear them. See Numbers 15:37ff. and Deuteronomy 6:4–6).

[12] Here, Yeshua gives an evaluation as to which *mitzvah* is the "umbrella" *mitzvah* of the Torah. In order to keep the *mitzvot* as God intended them to be kept, the rich ruler of Luke 18 should love God as his first priority in life, and should love his neighbor as himself. This man's attitude toward his wealth blocked his ability to do this. Such an umbrella *mitzvah* was a common thing for the rabbis to teach on during this period. One of many examples may be found in tractate *Makkot* 23–24 of the *Mishnah*, where we read, "Rabbi Salmai gave the following exposition: 613 commandments were given to Moses . . . then came David and made them compact into 11 commandments (Ps. 15) . . . then came Isaiah and reduced them to six commandments (Isa. 33:15) . . . then came Micah the prophet and reduced them to a compact three commandments (Mic. 6:8) . . . then came the prophet Habakkuk and reduced all the commandments to one, as it is written (Hab. 2:4), 'the just shall live by his faith.' "

[13] There is a difference in opinion among scholars as to whether Yeshua ate the Passover meal in accordance with the Essene calendar, or—as most people in

Israel did—in accordance with the more widely accepted lunar calendar. We will not address this issue, but only make the reader aware of it.

[14] John Fischer, "Jesus and Early Judaism," 7.

[15] Safrai lecture.

[16] Flusser, *Jesus in the Context of History*, 8.

Chapter Five

[1] John Fischer, "Paul in His Jewish Context," 13.

[2] John Fischer, "Paul in His Jewish Context," 13.

[3] In 1991, this subject was taken up in private conversations with Dr. John Fischer. I relay his opinion from these conversations.

[4] This incident shows that the Messianic Jewish community in Jerusalem continued to practice sacrificing at the Temple, as well as making the Nazirite vow, after Yeshua's death and resurrection.

[5] John Fischer, "The Place of Rabbinic Tradition," 4.

[6] *D'rashah* is Hebrew for a sermon based on a text from the Torah. In Acts 13:16–51, *Sha'ul* used historical narrative to highlight the actions of God in Jewish history. In verses 22 ff., Sha'ul emphasized the role of the promises to King David, and in verses 35–36, he gave both a Messianic and Pharisaic understanding of the resurrection. The emphases on historical narrative, the covenants, and the Exodus from Egypt (see v. 17) portray a strong Pharisaic and Messianic influence. His *d'rashah*, then, is his sermon based on his interpretation of Jewish history.

[7] Schiffman, *Who Was a Jew?*, 11.

[8] Schiffman, *Who Was a Jew?*, 10.

[9] Powlison, "Paul Kept the Law While with the Gentiles," 1.

[10] Powlison, "Paul Kept the Law While with the Gentiles," 1.

[11] Patrice Fischer, "Modern-Day Godfearers," 172.

[12] Powlison, "Misunderstood Passages," 7.

[13] Powlison, "Misunderstood Passages," 7.

[14] Abbott-Smith 432.

[15] See the United Bible Society's edition of *Brit Hadasha*, where Acts 18:7 reads, וביתו סמוך לבית הכנסת (*uveyto samukh l'veyt hak'neset*).

[16] Powlison, "Misunderstood Passages," 8.

[17] Tomson 234.

[18] Tomson 236.

[19] Tomson 55.

[20] Tomson 266.

[21] Santala 36.

[22] Parkes 15.

Chapter Six

[1] A klutz is a clumsy and slow-witted person.

[2] John and James also held some prominence among the *talmidim*, as evidenced by their participation in special events alongside Yeshua. By prominence, I do not mean a prideful, haughty role. Ideally, the *talmid hakham* had no such character. In particular, Yeshua taught that his greatest students were to be servants of all (see Matt. 23:11).

[3] *Shavu'ot* (The Feast of Weeks) is traditionally understood to be the time when Moses received the Torah from God on Mt. Sinai. The reception of the Holy Spirit during *Shavu'ot* is looked upon by some Messianic Jews as significant; there was a historic precedent for expecting God to give his people a great gift of grace and mercy, as he had done previously on this same occasion.

[4] Although the Scriptures quoted from the Proverbs are not strictly from the five books of Moses, they contribute to the whole picture of Second Temple Era theology. Indeed, the Five Books of Moses, the Former and Latter Prophets, and the Poetical Books (or Writings) appear to have been considered Scripture in Yeshua's day. To my knowledge, the only books that were in question regarding being considered Scripture were the Song of Songs and Ecclesiastes (*Kohelet*). *Shim'on*'s beliefs about God were built upon his total reading of Scripture, not just by his knowledge of the Torah.

[5] Some commentators add here that, from this point on, *Shim'on* realized he was free from the kosher dietary laws of the Torah, and began to eat non-kosher food. There is no proof of this in the New Covenant.

[69] Patrice Fischer, "Modern-Day Godfearers," 180.

Chapter Seven

[1] Louw and Nida 744.

[2] In Hebrew, *lamed vavnik* literally means a "thirty-sixer," and refers to the concept of God preserving thirty-six righteous Jews in each generation who, by their goods deeds and faith, stave off judgment on humanity.

[3] *Sh'khinah* is Hebrew for a physical manifestation of God's presence and glory, portrayed in rabbinic literature as being in both the Temple and the Tabernacle.

[4] The Septuagint is the ancient Greek translation of the Torah, done by Jews to help their non-Hebrew-reading kinsmen in Egypt learn the Torah, and probably to spread the news of one God to the Egyptian people of that time.

Chapter Eight

[1] *Shomer haTorah* or *shomer hamitzvot* indicates a Torah-observant person.

[2] *Beyt Hillel* and *Beyt Shammai* were respective movements of Pharisees from the Second Temple period in Israel. They were the two most popular wings of

Pharisaism. It is necessary to be familiar with them in order to see the proper historical context of Yeshua's life.

Chapter Nine

[1] "Common people" is a bit of a misnomer here. Israel's society, although certainly segmented, was not a feudal society with a landed aristocracy and a serf peasantry. Instead, the term "common people" refers to the people from rural areas of Israel who did not receive their education in Jerusalem. (This did not mean they were not well educated in the Torah. The agricultural, small merchant, and trade professions had many people in this category.

[2] Although the text relates this positive reaction here, the story unfolds and we see a negative reaction to Yeshua among his hometown citizens.

[3] There is some speculation that this Roman soldier may have been a *sebamenou ton Theon*, a Godfearer. It is an interesting speculation, and possibly a good guess, at his identity. However, there is no sure proof of this in the text (see Matt. 27:54).

[4] Again, this is probably a reference to the prophet spoken about in Deuteronomy 18:18.

Chapter Ten

[1] Neusner, *From Politics to Piety*, 49.

[2] Neusner, *Early Rabbinic Judaism*, 51.

[3] See Flavius Josephus, *Antiquities of the Jews*, 18:2:4, 460 in the Nelson edition.

[4] Both the New Testament and Josephus portray the Pharisees as still involved in politics, but without the influence they had in the previous century. This raises the question of the Zealots, whom Neusner sees as a Pharisaic element that broke off from the larger group because of their advocacy of a violent overthrow of the Roman government. Due to lack of attention afforded to this party in the New Testament, it will suffice to say that one of Yeshua's students appears to have been a one-time member of this group (see Luke 6:15 and Acts 1:13).

[5] Queen Alexandra, also known as Queen *Shlomit* (in Hebrew), was the wife of King Alexander Yanai. She inherited the throne after her husband's death. In fact, she and her brother, the Pharisaic sage *Shim'on ben Shetach*, ruled the Hasmonean kingdom for a few short years. Her reign was an era of unprecedented peace and authority for the Pharisees, who had previously experienced outright persecution from the Hasmonean throne.

[6] Neusner, *From Politics to Piety*, 8.

[7] John Fischer lecture.

[8] John Fischer, "Jesus and Early Judaism," 19.

[9] Although a large number of doctrinal differences existed between Yeshua and the priestly Temple officials—much more so than between Yeshua and any wing

of the Pharisees—this fact in itself would have been no reason to back harsh actions toward Yeshua. Politics became the major motivator.

[10] Neusner, *Early Rabbinic Judaism*, 67.

[11] Bright 463.

[12] Bright 464.

[13] Bright 464.

Chapter Eleven

[1] *Pax Romana* is the Latin phrase for "Roman Peace." This was the ideal of all of ancient Rome's political policies. It meant that all peoples and lands in the Roman Empire must accept Rome's political authority over them, and do nothing that would endanger this authority, either locally or abroad.

[2] Davies 89.

[3] Pritz 20.

[4] Pritz 45.

[5] Williamson 137.

[6] Williamson 137.

[7] Schifmann, *Who Was a Jew?* The entire book takes up this subject.

[8] Tomson 2.

Chapter Twelve

[1] In addition, there is the concept of *g'milut hasadim*, which was taught as one of the pillars of faithful Jewish existence (see *Avot* 1:2). *G'milut hasadim* is close to *rachamim* in substance. It means the doing of good deeds as a reflection of one's devotion to God.

[2] See Luke 1:1 and Acts 1:1

Chapter Thirteen

[1] Patrice Fischer discusses this issue in "Modern-Day Godfearers."

[2] Ritual bath

Chapter Fourteen

[1] God himself promised in Jeremiah 31:33–34, that he would cause all Israel to internalize the Torah: " 'I will put My law within them and on their heart I will write it; and I will be their God, and they shall be My people. And they shall not teach again, each man his neighbor and each man his brother, saying, "Know the Lord," for they shall all know Me, from the least of them to the greatest of them,' declares the Lord" (NASB).

GLOSSARY

- B.C.E. and C.E.—Respectively, these terms stand for "Before the Common Era" (B.C.E., commonly B.C.) and "Common Era" (C.E., commonly A.D.).

- *Beyt Hillel* (Hebrew, בית הילל)—the school of thought of the Pharisees who looked to the first century sage Hillel as a main source for their way of formulating *halakhah*

- *Beyt Shammai* (Hebrew, בית שמאי)—the school of thought of the Pharisees who looked to the sage Shammai as a main source for their way of formulating *halakhah*

- *B'rit Milah* (Hebrew, ברית מילה)—Jewish ritual circumcision

- *Halakhah* (Hebrew, הלכה)—Jewish religious/legal code. In this book it will mainly refer to how the *mitzvot* of the Torah were developed for application in daily life.

- *Kashrut* (Hebrew, כשרות)—the kosher dietary laws

- *Kohen* (Hebrew, כהן)—a priest, a descendant of Aaron

- *Mitzvah*; pl. *mitzvot* (Hebrew, מצווה / מצוות)—a biblical commandment found in the Torah

- *Rav* (Hebrew, רב)—Rabbi

- Sanhedrin (Hebrew, סנהדרין)—the term designating the rabbis and priests who made up the supreme legislative and judicial body of Israel's Jewish community in Second Temple times

- *Shabbat* (Hebrew, שבת)— Sabbath, the seventh-day rest

- *Sha'ul* (Hebrew, שאול)—Saul (Paul)

- *Shim'on* (Hebrew, שמעון)—Peter's given name

- *Talmidim* (Hebrew, תלמידים)—students, disciples

- Talmud—the collection of ancient Rabbinic writings consisting of the *Mishnah* and the *Gemara*, constituting the basis of religious authority in Judaism

- *Tanakh* (Hebrew, תנ״ך)—Hebrew acronym for the Torah (Pentateuch), the *Nevi'im* (Prophets), and the *K'tuvim* (Writings); commonly known as the "Old" Testament

- *Tzaddik* (Hebrew, צדיק)—the word used to describe a man who lived a strict, Torah-observant lifestyle and whose life was an example to others of serving and loving God

- *Ya'akov* (Hebrew, יעקוב)—James' (half-brother to Yeshua) given name

- Yeshua (Hebrew, ישוע)—This is the Hebrew name for Jesus, the name by which he was called during his lifetime. The Galilean pronunciation of his time rendered his name *Yeshu* when spoken.

- *Yochanan ben Zavdai* (Hebrew, יוחנן בן זבדאי)—John, son of Zebedee

BIBLIOGRAPHY

Abbott-Smith, G., ed. *Greek Lexicon of the New Testament*. London: United Bible Societies, 1971.

Aland, Kurt, et al., eds. *The Greek New Testament*. Stuttgart, Germany: Deutsche Bibelgesellschaft, 1993.

Alcalay, Reuven, ed. *Milon Ivri-Angli Shalem*. Bridgeport: Prayer Book, 1974.

Arndt, W. F. and Gingrich, F.W., eds. *A Greek-English Lexicon of the New Testament and Other Early Christian Literature*. Chicago: U of Chicago P, 1988.

Avigad, N. *The Herodian Quarter in Jerusalem*. Jerusalem: Keter, 1990.

Bacchiocchi, Samuel. *To Sunday from Sabbath*. Rome: Pontifical Gregorian, 1977.

Bahat, Dan. *The Atlas of Biblical Jerusalem*. Jerusalem: Carta, 1994.

Ben Isaiah, Rabbi Abraham and Rabbi Benjamin Sharfman, eds. *The Pentateuch and Rashi's Commentary*. 5 vols. Brooklyn: S. S. & R., 1950.

Bettenson, Henry, ed. *Documents of the Early Church*. London: Oxford UP, 1972.

Berkovits, Eliezer. *Not in Heaven*. Hoboken: KTAV, 1983.

Berkowitz, Ariel and D'vorah. *Take Hold*. Jerusalem: First Fruits of Zion, 1998.

———. *Torah Rediscovered*. Jerusalem: First Fruits of Zion, 1996.

Bivin, David. "The Miraculous Catch." *Jerusalem Perspective* 5:2 (March–April 1992): 7–10.

Bivin, David and Roy Blizzard. *Understanding the Difficult Words of Jesus*. Arcadia: Makor, 1983.

Brenton, Lancelot, ed. *The Septuagint with Apocrypha: Greek and English*. Peabody: Hendrickson, 1992.

Bright, John. *A History of Israel*. Philadelphia: Westminster, 1981.

Cohen, Chuck. *Tanach Roots of the New Covenant*. Jerusalem: King of Kings, 1995.

Danby, Herbert, trans. *The Mishnah*. New York: Oxford UP, 1987.

Davies, J. G. *The Early Christian Church*. Grand Rapids: Baker, 1980.

DeVaux, Roland. *Ancient Israel*. 2 vols. New York: McGraw-Hill, 1965.

Edersheim, Alfred. *The Life and Times of Jesus the Messiah*. Grand Rapids: Eerdmans, 1971.

Eidelberg, Paul. *Israel's Return and Restoration: The Secret of Her Conquest, from a Discourse of Dr. Chaim Zimmerman*. Jerusalem: Feldheim, 1987.

Epstein, Rabbi I., ed. *The Babylonian Talmud*, London: Soncino, 1972.

Evans, Craig and Peter Flint, eds. *Eschatology, Messianism and the Dead Sea Scrolls*. Grand Rapids: Eerdmans, 1997.

Falk, Harvey. *Jesus the Pharisee*. New York: Paulist, 1985.

Fischer, John. "Jesus and Early Judaism." *Messianic Jewish Outreach* 9:4 (Summer 1990).

————. Lecture. Medicine Lake Lutheran Seminary. Minneapolis. 11 July 1991.

————. "Paul in His Jewish Context." Unpublished essay, 1987.

————. *The Olive Tree Connection.* Downers Grove: InterVarsity, 1978.

———— and ed. "The Place of Rabbinic Tradition in a Messianic Jewish Lifestyle." *The Enduring Paradox: Exploratory Essays in Messianic Judaism.* Baltimore: Lederer/Messianic Jewish Publishers, 2000. 145–170

Fischer, Patrice. "Modern-Day Godfearers: A Biblical Model for Gentile Participation in Messianic Congregations." *The Enduring Paradox: Exploratory Essays in Messianic Judaism,* Ed. John Fischer. Baltimore: Lederer/Messianic Jewish Publishers, 2000. 171–181.

Flannery, Edward. *The Anguish of the Jews.* New York: Paulist, 1985.

Flusser, David. *Jesus in the Context of History.* New York: Herder and Herder, 1969.

————. *Jewish Sources in Early Christianity.* Tel Aviv, Israel: MOD Books, 1993.

————. *Yahadut Umekorot HaNatzrut.* Tel Aviv: Hakibbutz Ha'artzi, 1979.

Frankovic, Joseph. "The Nature of Jesus' Task." *Jerusalem Perspective* 52 (July–September 1997): 12.

————. "Stewards of God's Keys." *Jerusalem Perspective* 50 (January-March 1996): 26–31.

Friedman, David. "Assessing the Jerusalem Religious Authorities' Reaction to the Message of Messianic Judaism." Unpublished essay, 1989.

————. "The Relationship of Yeshua and the First Century CE Messianic Jewish Community to the *Mitzvot* of the Mosaic Covenant: Demonstrating a Torah-observant Lifestyle." Diss. California Graduate School of Theology, 1992.

Goodrich, E. W. and J. R. Kohlenberger. *The NIV Complete Concordance.* Grand Rapids: Zondervan, 1981.

Grant, Michael. *The Jews in the Roman World.* New York: Scribners and Sons, 1973.

Hagner, Donald. *The Jewish Reclamation of Jesus.* Grand Rapids: Zondervan, 1984.

Hertz, J. H., ed. *The Pentateuch and Haftorah.* London: Soncino, 1987.

Kehati, Pinhas, comm. *Mishnah.* 15 vols. Jerusalem: Maor Wallach, 1994.

Lachs, Samuel. *A Rabbinic Commentary on the New Testament.* Hoboken: KTAV, 1987.

Lapide, Pinhas. *The Resurrection of Jesus.* Minneapolis: Augsburg, 1983.

———— and Peter Stuhlmacher. *Paul, Rabbi and Apostle,* Minneapolis: Augsburg, 1984.

Lee, Bernard. *The Galilean Jewishness of Jesus.* New York: Paulist, 1988.

Liddell, H. and R. Scott, comps. *A Greek-English Lexicon.* Oxford: Clarendon, 1968.

Longenecker, Richard. *The Christology of Early Jewish Christianity.* Grand Rapids: Baker, 1981.

Louw, J. and E. Nida, eds. *Greek-English Lexicon.* New York: United Bible Societies, 1988.

Mason, Steve. *Josephus and the New Testament.* Peabody: Hendrickson, 1992.

Morgenstern, Benjamin. *A Companion to Pirke Avot.* Bet El, Israel: Gefen, 1983.

Mounce, Robert. *The Relationship of Jesus and the Law.* Ann Arbor: U Microfilms, 1958.

Mulder, M. J., ed. *Mikra.* Minneapolis: Fortress, 1990.

Nanos, Mark. *The Mystery of Romans.* Minneapolis: Fortress, 1996.

Nelson, T. and Sons, eds. *Flavius Josephus' Antiquities of the Jews,* London: Nelson and Sons, 1892.

Nestle, Eberhard and Erwin and Kurt Aland, eds. *Novum Testamentum Graece.* Stuttgart, Germany: Deutsche Bibelstiftung, 1979.

Neusner, Jacob. *Early Rabbinic Judaism.* Leiden, The Netherlands: Brill. 1969.

———. *From Politics to Piety.* Englewood Cliffs: Prentice-Hall, 1973.

Nun, Mendel. *The Sea of Galilee and Its Fishermen in the New Testament.* Kibbutz Ein Gev, Israel: Kibbutz Ein Gev, 1989.

Parkes, James. *Judaism and Christianity.* London: Gollancz, 1948.

Powlison, Aryeh. "Misunderstood Passages." Unpublished essay, 1987.

———. "Paul Kept the Law While with the Gentiles," Unpublished essay, 1985.

Pritchard, James R., ed. *The Ancient Middle East.* 2 vols. Princeton: Princeton UP, 1975.

Pritz, Ray. *Nazarene Jewish Christianity.* Jerusalem: Magnes, 1988.

Richman, Chaim. *The Holy Temple of Jerusalem.* Jerusalem: The Temple Institute and Carta, 1997.

Riggans, Walter. *Jesus Ben Joseph.* Tunbridge Wells, U.K.: Monarch, 1993.

Ritmeyer, Leen and Kathleen. *Secrets of Jerusalem's Temple Mount.* Washington: Biblical Archaeology Society, 1998.

Rodkinson, Michael, eds. *Babylonian Talmud.* 10 vols. Boston: New Talmud Publication Society, 1916.

Roth, Cecil, ed. *Encyclopædia Judaica.* Jerusalem: Keter, 1971.

Ryrie, Charles, ed. *The Ryrie Study Bible.* Chicago: Moody, 1978.

Safrai, Rabbi Shmuel. "The Torah Observance of Yeshua." Lecture. Jerusalem. 16 Dec. 1996.

Safrai, Shmuel and Menachem Stern, eds. *The Jewish People in the First Century,* Vol. 2. Philadelphia: Fortress, 1974. 2 vols.

Santala, Risto. *Paul, The Man and the Teacher in the Light of Jewish Sources.* Jerusalem: Keren Ahavat Meshihit, 1995.

———. "The Jerusalem School and Its Theory." *Jerusalem Perspective* 54 (July-September 1998): 32–33.

Scherman, Nosson, trans. *The Complete Art Scroll Siddur.* Brooklyn: Mesorah, 1984.

Schiffman, Lawrence. *From Text to Tradition.* Hoboken: KTAV, 1991.

———. *Who Was a Jew?* Hoboken: KTAV, 1985.

Scholem, Gershom. *The Messianic Idea in Judaism*. New York: Schocken, 1974.

Shisha Sidray Mishnah.

Stern, David, ed. and trans. *Complete Jewish Bible*. Clarksville, Md.: Jewish New Testament Publications, 1998.

Tomson, Peter. *Paul and the Jewish Law*. Minneapolis: Fortress, 1990.

The Torah. Philadelphia: Jewish Publication Society, 1962.

Torah, Nevi'im, Ketuvim. Jerusalem: Qoren.

Urbach, Ephraim E. *The Sages*. Jerusalem: Magnes, 1979.

Vermes, Geza. *The Religion of Jesus the Jew*. Minneapolis: Fortress, 1993.

Von Soden, Wolfram. *The Ancient Orient*. Grand Rapids: Eerdmans, 1985.

Williamson, G.R., ed. *Eusebius' History of the Church*. Baltimore: Penguin, 1965.

Young, Brad. *Jesus the Jewish Theologian*. Peabody: Hendrickson, 1995.

———. *Paul the Jewish Theologian*. Peabody: Hendrickson, 1997.